WOMEN IN THEIR SPEECH COMMUNITIES

Women in Their Speech Communities

New Perspectives on Language and Sex

Editors: Jennifer Coates and Deborah Cameron

LONGMAN
LONDON AND NEW YORK

Longman Group UK Limited,
Longman House, Burnt Mill, Harlow,
Essex CM20 2JE, England
and Associated Companies throughout the world.

*Published in the United States of America
by Longman Inc., New York*

© Longman Group UK Limited 1988

First published 1989
Third impression 1991

British Library Cataloguing in Publication Data

Women in their speech communities: new
perspectives on language and sex.
1. Women – Language – Social aspects
I. Coates, Jennifer   II. Cameron, Deborah
306′.4   P120.W66

ISBN 0-582-00969-3

Library of Congress Cataloging in Publication Data

Women in their speech communities: new
perspectives on language and sex/editors,
Jennifer Coates and Deborah Cameron.
p.   cm.
Bibliography: p.
Includes index.
ISBN 0-582-00969-3
1. Language and languages – Sex
differences. 2. Women – Language.
I. Coates, Jennifer. II. Cameron, Deborah, 1958–.
P120.S48W65   1988
408′.8042 – dc19   87-34179
CIP

Set in Linotron 202 10/11pt Times
Printed in Malaysia
by Vinlin Press Sdn. Bhd.,
Sri Petaling, Kuala Lumpur.

Contents

Preface

This collection of papers is a contribution to the field of research on language and sex. Although 'language and gender' might in some sense be more accurate, since we are dealing with a social rather than a biological category, the term *gender* has a technical meaning for linguists which has caused many writers to prefer the term *sex*.

The book is organised in two main Parts: the first deals with the so-called 'quantitative paradigm' in sociolinguistics, that is, work on phonological and grammatical variation in the general tradition of William Labov; the second Part takes as its focus the study of a wider 'communicative style', drawing on approaches from discourse analysis and the ethnography of speaking. Since the two traditions are rather different and have tended to throw up slightly different issues (though inevitably there is a certain amount of overlap which readers will doubtless perceive for themselves) we have chosen not to provide a single, general introduction, but rather to introduce each Part separately. The purpose of our two introductory pieces is to set out approaches and areas of debate which will then be taken up by the contributors in each section.

The purpose of this preface, on the other hand, is to set out the objectives of the collection as a whole. These are suggested by our chosen subtitle, *New Perspectives on Language and Sex*, and we want now to explain why 'new perspectives' is appropriate.

The first reason relates to the chronological development of the field of enquiry we are concerned with. It is now around 15 years since publications began to mushroom, and thus to bring the whole subject of sex differences in language to the attention of a wider audience in the disciplines. Robin Lakoff's essay *Language and Women's Place*, for instance, had its first publication in 1973; the influential collection edited by Thorne and Henley, *Language and Sex: Difference and Dominance*, appeared two years later in 1975. Since then, a considerable body of work has accumulated, and it is commonplace to find the topic featured on graduate and undergraduate courses. In other words, the field is sufficiently well established to make reflection and reassessment of earlier work possible – reassessment, that is, in the light of 'new perspectives' on both language and the nature of gender relations. The papers in this volume are designed to further the process of reflection; some, indeed, are explicitly addressed to theoretical questions raised by early research.

A second reason for speaking of 'new perspectives' is that we have collected together research on a range of speech communities which have not so far featured in the literature on sex and language. The collections most often used by researchers and teachers alike (such as Thorne & Henley 1975; McConnell-Ginet, Borker & Furman 1980; Thorne, Kramarae & Henley 1983) focus mainly on communities in the USA, and the authors represented are also mostly North American. This, by contrast, is a *British* collection, and it attempts to represent, as far as possible given limited space, the linguistic diversity of British speech communities. We are particularly pleased to be able to include work on British minority women from groups as different as Afro-Caribbeans in the West Midlands, Welsh speakers in the Port Talbot area and Gujarati speakers in the London borough of Brent. This is unfortunately still an under-researched area, and we can only hope that the neglect it has suffered will soon be a thing of the past.

Finally, we are delighted to be presenting a volume consisting entirely of contributions by women linguists living and working in Britain. While several of our contributors are already well known, others are relative newcomers to the field and some are publishing here for the first time. We are aware, moreover, of other women doing interesting research which we have been unable to include. All this testifies to a high level of interest in the field of language and sex, as well as to the increasing visibility of women in linguistics. We think it augurs well for the continuing development of 'new perspectives' for future research.

J.C.
D.C.

Part One

Language and Sex in the Quantitative
Paradigm

Chapter 1

Introduction

Deborah Cameron

1. Some preliminaries

This introduction attempts to place in context four essays on sex differences in linguistic behaviour at the level of phonology and to a lesser extent grammar. While research on this topic undoubtedly represents a legitimate academic endeavour from the point of view of the pursuit of knowledge, it should be made clear that the framework in which I shall discuss it is to a very large extent a political one. The work which women are currently undertaking on language and sex must reflect, to a greater or lesser extent, the influence of feminism over the past two decades. Feminism has foregrounded issues of gender difference and male dominance in society; it has prompted a concern with putting women 'on the map' and a critical reappraisal of pre- and nonfeminist research. Accordingly, my discussion will focus on this feminist project of 'redressing the balance', as it has manifested itself in one particular academic field.[1]

2. The quantitative paradigm

All the essays which make up this section either deal with or exemplify an approach to the study of linguistic variation which has come to be known as the **quantitative paradigm**. Adherents of this approach adopt varying methods with regard to the collection and manipulation of data, but what defines their work as part of the paradigm is their use of the analytic concept of the **linguistic variable**. It is this concept which allows sociolinguists to quantify their data and to make correlations between linguistic and social structures.[2]

A brief example will illustrate the method. Perhaps the best-known exponent of the quantitative paradigm, William Labov, carried out a famous study in three New York City department stores (Labov 1972a). He was interested in the linguistic variable (r) – that is, the fact that in New York City r in postvocalic position can either be pronounced [ɹ] or not at all (these alternatives are known as **variants**). Labov asked sales staff in the three stores questions which elicited the answer *fourth floor* – a phrase in which the variable appears twice. Every time a subject pronounced the [ɹ] variant he gave them a score of 1; each time the zero variant was produced he awarded a score of 0. He was thus able to arrive at an overall numerical score for the speakers in each store. The stores he had chosen were ranked by social status from a high-class establishment to a fairly downmarket one. This ranking was reflected in the scores for (r): in New York City it is prestigious to use the pronunciation [ɹ], and Labov found that the higher the status of the store, the higher the score of its staff for (r). A more detailed study of New York City speakers confirmed that the variable (r) was 'socially stratified', that is, a speaker's (r) score could be correlated with their class.

The social stratification of (r) is one example of a **sociolinguistic pattern** – a statistical regularity which connects linguistic to nonlinguistic variables. It has been found empirically that this regularity is not peculiar to New York City but typical of linguistic variation in urban speech communities generally. For example, Peter Trudgill in his pioneering British study of Norwich English (1974a) found that the variable (ing) – whether the suffix in items like *walking* is realised as [ɪŋ] or [ɪn] – behaved much like (r) in New York City. The salient linguistic variables differ from place to place, but the social stratification pattern recurs.

The early phase of the quantitative paradigm was characterised by a concern to demonstrate a small number of sociolinguistic patterns in a wide range of speech communities. Social stratification is only one of the patterns this research uncovered. Another correlation which regularly appeared was that between rising scores on prestige variants and increasing formality of the speech situation (this is usually referred to as **'styleshift'**). A further important sociolinguistic pattern was associated with the *sex* of the speaker. When informants in each social class were subdivided by sex, it was typically found that women's scores were closer to the standard than those of men of the same status.

This particular finding about sex differences was reported in an impressive number of communities, including: rural New

England (Fischer 1958); North Carolina (Levine & Crockett 1966; Anshen 1969); New York City (Labov 1966); Detroit (Shuy, Wolfram & Riley 1967); Norwich (Trudgill 1974a); Glasgow (Macaulay 1977); and Edinburgh (Romaine 1978). Not surprisingly, it came to be regarded by sociolinguists as an almost unchallengeable fact about the structure of sociolinguistic variation. Their attention was therefore turned to the matter of explanation: the pattern clearly existed, but why did it exist? Why should women use more standard pronunciation than men?

In fact, the answer to this question and the implications of it are still being debated, and the essays in this section are contributions to the continuing debate. The matter, in other words, is not yet settled; the various competing proposals that have been made about it will be reviewed in much more detail in Chapter 2. What does need to be pointed out here, though, is that by the mid-1970s an explanation of sorts had emerged which commanded widespread agreement and respect. This explanation, championed by the extremely influential Labov and the increasingly respected Trudgill, related women's more correct or careful speech to their social role as females. This role involved paying attention to appearances and superficial aspects of behaviour to a higher degree than was expected of men (language 'refinement' being an aspect of this). It involved responsibility for transmitting the norms of speech to children (something which would make women especially sensitive to correctness and encourage them to 'set a good example') and finally, it denied women the opportunity to pursue social status through *work* in the same way men did (the implication being that if women wished to improve their social standing they would be obliged to focus on markers like accent).

At the time of Labov and Trudgill's actual field research – the late 1960s – this all must have seemed reasonable enough. But it was soon to be challenged by feminists who criticised almost every aspect of the quantitative paradigm's dealings with women. The reasons for such feminist dissatisfaction have, unfortunately, very often been misunderstood (especially, it seems, by Trudgill: see Trudgill 1983: Ch. 9), and it is therefore necessary to place them in their wider context. Feminists were not and are not arguing that 'anything you can do we can do better' – including nonstandard pronunciation! Rather, their point has been that methodology, measuring instruments and scoring systems, theoretical assumptions and individual interpretations have been, in sociolinguistics as elsewhere, riddled with bias and stereotype; and that this bias must not be ignored, because studies of 'differ-

ence' are not just disinterested quests for the truth, but in an
unequal society inevitably have a political dimension.

3. Sociolinguistics and the feminist critique

3.1 The politics of difference

The description and explanation of gender difference, not only
in language but in any sphere whatever, is not a straightforward
enterprise; with the emergence of a feminist perspective in the
academy as well as outside it, the topic has been rapidly and
explicitly politicised. We must remember, of course, that to
feminist minds it always *was* implicitly a political question. For
sex – like race – is an area of social relations where *dominance*
has invariably been justified by *difference*. Male investigators
have devoted endless time and trouble to the quest for significant
differences between the sexes on which to base their unequal
treatment of women.

Thus to take two nineteenth-century examples, it was widely
contended that women should not have civil rights (e.g. to own
property, to vote, etc.) because they lacked the necessary
reasoning faculties. Women's status as legal minors could be
justified on the grounds of their 'childlike' mental inferiority (we
hear analogous arguments about black people from today's white
South Africans). Similarly, as late as 1873 it was argued that
higher education for women would shrivel their reproductive
organs and render them sterile. Both these assertions, ridiculous
as they now seem, were put forward at the time as 'scientific fact'
and the results of 'research'.[3] And while discussions of who uses
what linguistic variant may well seem less immediately unjust and
partisan, these examples from the past should serve to remind
us just what is at stake in research on gender difference. The
hidden agenda is female inferiority – or put another way,
continued male dominance.

The feminist critique of the social sciences which began to gain
momentum in the late 1960s has made it its business to seek out
and challenge this hidden agenda in social research. The quantitative paradigm in sociolinguistics has by no means escaped the
critique's attentions, and we may look at the complaints which
have been levelled against it.

3.2 Invisible, peripheral and 'deviant' women

The first complaint made by feminist critics concerns the 'invis-
ibility' of women: the way they are excluded from research or at
best, defined as peripheral and 'deviant'. Sociolinguistics, at least

in Britain, inherited a tradition of work in dialectology from which women informants were almost completely absent. The Survey of English Dialects provides little information on women speakers, because in the words of Harold Orton – words for which he put forward no evidence at all – 'men speak vernacular more frequently, more consistently and more genuinely than women' (Orton, 1962: 15).

While major sociolinguistic studies have usually sampled the speech of both sexes, some classic studies have excluded women, the most notorious being Labov's work with Black peer groups (Labov 1972a). The speech of men can apparently stand for speech in general, whereas we do not find 'representative' studies of all-female groups. The net result is that we know less than we might about women's speech. Labov has asserted in his defence that 'males are the chief exemplars of the vernacular culture' (Labov et. al, 1968: 41): but as Conklin (1973) points out 'no conclusive evidence has been presented'.

In any case, it all depends what you take the vernacular culture to *be*. As many feminists have observed, there is a circularity here whereby men's behaviour is taken as a yardstick and when women behave differently they are perceived to fall short (just as, if we define 'average height' as average *male* height, this will automatically define the majority of women as 'below average'). If vernacular culture is defined as a property of gangs whose main activities are fighting and 'hanging out', and only those iinguistic variables are examined which are salient to gang-members, then it is obvious that women's activities and language will not be described as 'vernacular'.

In their paper 'Some problems in the sociolinguistic explanation of sex differences' (Ch. 2), Cameron and Coates discuss a number of instances where women in quantitative sociolinguistic studies have been measured using instruments designed for men. This paper suggests that both traditional socioeconomic indices and conventional criteria for network strength, as well as definitions of vernacular culture, may well be inapplicable to the particular circumstances of women, and that by using them investigators risk losing important information and distorting the results which they do obtain.

3.3 Explaining difference: stereotypes

Both Cameron and Coates and Margaret Deuchar (Ch. 3) draw attention to the inadequate and stereotypical accounts which have been marshalled to explain the classic sociolinguistic pattern of sex differentiation. This is the second main theme of the feminist critique: that researchers attempting to explain, as opposed to merely describing, gender difference, frequently resort to invoking sex stereotypes.

It is worth sorting out some confusions about the term **stereotype** and its meaning in this context. Stereotypes need be neither false nor negative (though many, of course, are both); so what is it about them that people find objectionable?

To stereotype someone is to interpret their behaviour, personality and so on in terms of a set of common-sense attributions which are applied to whole groups (e.g. 'Italians are excitable'; 'Black people are good at sport'). One crucial point about this is that the atributions are overgeneralised; even when they are not absolutely false they are only partially true, since they imply that the characteristic in question is found in all members of the group in question. Individual differences are at best overlooked and at worst denied – which is both simplistic and insulting to those concerned.

It must be said, too, that stereotyping is most often suffered by minority groups, i.e. those who are socially subordinate and/or stigmatised. In the case of gender, therefore, it is women who get stereotyped. Simone de Beauvoir, author of the ground-breaking *Second Sex*, observed that it was considered perfectly all right to say to a woman 'you think such and such because you are a woman' but ludicrous to retort 'well, you think such and such because you are a man!' Everything about women is traced back to their sex alone. Thorne, Kramarae and Henley (1983: 14) put this point very aptly in relation to social scientific investigation when they say that 'in traditional research . . . women are more often conceptualised in a singular condition, while men are allowed an individualism that transcends gender'. One thing which feminist critics of social science have insisted on is that women cannot just be lumped together wholesale; attention must be paid to the differences between them.

The two empirical case studies published here – Viv Edward's study of Black speakers in Dudley (Ch. 4) and Beth Thomas's study of Welsh speakers in Pont-rhyd-y-fen (Ch. 5) – are very concerned with different women's differing experiences and with exploding inappropriate stereotypes. It is no coincidence that both authors use a methodology – the 'social network' approach – which is very sensitive to individual and small group differences. Previous studies in this vein (Milroy 1980; Cheshire 1982; Russell 1982) have succeeded in showing that the 'classic' sociolinguistic pattern whereby women are more standard in their speech than men is indeed an overgeneralisation – counterexamples do exist.

Milroy, for example, studied three working-class communities in Belfast. If she had simply quantified the overall scores for 'women' and 'men', her results would have reaffirmed the usual pattern; but by looking at the variables of age, neighbourhood and the type of social network different speakers participated in, she discovered that in one group, young people from the Clonard district, women had higher vernacular scores than their male peers. This could be explained as a consequence of local patterns of interaction and employment; because of the conditions in the area, young Clonard women had tighter-knit networks than either young Clonard men or women from the other districts.

This is a subtly different type of explanation from the kind which more traditional researchers favour. Instead of focussing on a supposed 'common denominator' of female experience – domestic and childcare responsibilities – and trying to use that as a blanket explanation, Milroy studied the place of various groups of women in specific speech communities. Instead of discussing sex difference in terms of psychology or 'attitudes' (women are more sensitive to norms of correctness; women feel more socially insecure) Milroy concentrates on material factors such as the employment opportunities open to the sexes.

Milroy's example is followed by Viv Edwards and Beth Thomas in their contributions to this part of the book. Edwards, for instance, is concerned to challenge the received wisdom that patois speakers in British Black communities are predominantly 'angry male underachievers'. Although men do score higher overall on an index of eleven frequently occurring patois features, Edwards points out that 'many of the most competent patois speakers were women'. She also relates the overall finding to prevailing local conditions, especially the high rate of Black male unemployment which ensures that Black men who are unemployed interact with each other much more than with white outsiders. (This network-strengthening effect of unemployment is the reverse of Belfast as reported by Milroy: unemployed Belfast people have *weaker* networks. What this reversal indicates is that sociolinguistic patterns are highly localised; one simply cannot generalise from majority groups organised around paid work to minority groups where, deplorably, unemployment is the norm and not the exception. And there are clear analogies with the situation of unwaged women here too.) Finally, Edwards makes telling use of qualitative data on individual speakers to challenge sex stereotypes. As she says, 'when we focus on the overall picture, we risk losing sight of the individuals on whom the study is based'.

Beth Thomas's essay also challenges conventional wisdom. Thomas has studied the East Glamorgan dialect of Welsh in the small community of Pont-rhyd-y-fen, and has found one local variant, [ɛ:], retained only in the speech of the older women – men and young people do not use it. This, argues Thomas, is connected with local network structures; in Pont-rhyd-y-fen older women have the strongest neighbourhood ties, despite the fact (or indeed, *because* of it) that for the most part they fulfil an entirely traditional female role working inside the home. It seems that female domesticity need not lead to the kind of anxiety and insecurity about status which allegedly causes women to aspire to 'correct' standard pronunciation; nor is it inevitably a concomitant of weak social networks.

Thomas observes that there is significant variation among the older women themselves, as well as between them and other local residents. She links this to membership of particular chapels. Her findings show once again how important it is to examine the conditions of people's lives at a very local level and to avoid masculist biasses about what is culturally important. Chapel in Pont-rhyd-y-fen is a markedly female sphere, and in this case the site of vernacular culture (where local vernacular forms, elsewhere long since lost, are retained). How often do we associate 'vernacular culture' with the religious practices of older women rather than the activities of male adolescents on the mean streets of the inner city? Yet the fact that women are excluded from some areas of popular culture does not prevent them forming enclaves elsewhere.

All discussions of how women operate in speech communities must, however, be aware of women's more general social and political position as a subordinate group. To be sure, women's subordination is manifested in varying ways among different groups; in different times, places, classes, ethnic groups . . . but it is all too easy to lose sight of the *fact* of subordination and describe 'sex roles' (in the manner of so many male sociolinguists) as 'natural', 'facts of life', difference not inequality.

Whereas many influential researchers have chosen to explain the more standard speech of women as a marker of their identification with a particular role, feminists have stressed the importance of sex inequality. Early feminist writers on this subject couched their accounts in terms of oppressive social expectations forcing women to be circumspect and 'talk like ladies' whether they liked it or not (see for instance the discussion and citations in Thorne & Henley 1975: 17–18). But recently there has been something of a rethink. In her essay 'A pragmatic account of women's use of standard speech' (Ch. 3), Margaret Deuchar suggests that the use of more standard pronunciation and grammar may be a more positively chosen strategy which allows women to boost their self-esteem ('face') *without* offending or threatening their social superordinates, men. Deuchar's assumption is that any useful account of gender differentiation in language must explicitly discuss the question of **power**: a point which can hardly be overemphasised.

4. Summary

We can sum up this introductory discussion, and indeed the whole section dealing with the quantitative paradigm, by listing the most important points that seem to emerge and which need to be considered in future research.

1. The quantitative paradigm's major finding concerning sex difference – that women's pronunciation is on average closer to the standard than men's – is widespread but not universal or unchallengeable.

2. Traditional sociolinguistic methods and measuring instruments have frequently been designed for male speakers and may not be maximally well adapted for female informants. Care needs to be taken to select informants of both sexes and to investigate all-female as well as all-male groups; to design non-linguistic criteria such as social class, network strength, etc. in ways that are applicable to both sexes; and to avoid definitions of important concepts (e.g. vernacular culture) that mean women are automatically excluded.

3. Explanations of sex differences in linguistic behaviour have too often been based on common-sense sex stereotypes. This tendency must be corrected in two ways:

    (a) more attention needs to be paid to social and linguistic differences within gender groups; neither men nor women form homogeneous categories whose members live in the same conditions, think and act in identical ways.

    (b) On the other hand it must be acknowledged that many of the differences that exist between the sexes are a direct or indirect result of inequality between them. Researchers must take explicit account of this and reflect on the political character of sex-difference research in a society which is still profoundly unequal.

The essays in this section, both theoretical and empirical, are written with these points very much in mind. Taken as a group, they cannot be said to exemplify any one 'line' on language and sex; the debate is still very much 'work in progress'. What all the contributors share, however, is a critical perspective on the quantitative paradigm in which they work, and a commitment to fuller and richer accounts of the behaviour of women in their speech commmunities.

Notes

1. I do not wish to imply, however, that my political perspective is necessarily shared by individual contributors, who will doubtless indicate their own outlook in what they have written.
2. Some linguists, notably Trudgill (1978), would equate all sociolinguistics with the quantitative paradigm. In this volume we take the view Trudgill argues against, i.e. that the quantitative paradigm is only one approach within sociolinguistics (others include ethnography of speaking, discourse and conversation analysis). Thus, all the papers in this book are 'sociolinguistic' in orientation.
3. The source for these and many other examples is Ehrenreich & English (1979).

Chapter 2

Some problems in the sociolinguistic explanation of sex differences[1]

Deborah Cameron & Jennifer Coates

1. Introduction

In this chapter, we shall be concerned with what we are calling 'sociolinguistic explanation'. Let us emphasise that we are not denying the existence of sex differences in language use. Awareness of such differences goes back a long way; it is part of our folklinguistic heritage. Modern sociolinguistic studies have improved on folklinguistics, however, giving us a clearer picture of linguistic variation in general. Variation associated with the sex of the speaker is now well documented in communities as different as New York, Mombasa, Belfast and Norwich. But the main goal of these quantitative studies has been the collection and analysis of data on linguistic variation: sociolinguists are not primarily concerned with the reasons for such variation, and their methodology is not usually designed to probe such issues. Sociolinguistics has dealt, therefore, with the *what* of sex differences, but has it dealt so well with the *why*? Do the conventional explanations given in sociolinguistic analysis stand up to scrutiny? That is the question we want to address.

Before turning to the problem of explanation, it is as well to outline what is being explained. In the case of sex difference, the major finding is well known: women on average deviate less from the prestige standard than men. This is true for a fair number of cultures, though not all; exceptions include Malagasy (Keenan 1974) and certain Muslim communities (Labov, personal communication). In modern urban societies it is typically true for every social class.

Three main explanations have been proposed for this persistent difference: one in terms of **conservatism** (women stick to older forms because they are more conservative); one in terms of **status** (women speak more 'correctly' because they are sensitive to the social connotations of speech); and one in terms of **solidarity** (women do not experience the same pressure as men to adhere to vernacular norms). We will take these explanations one at a time.

2. Conservatism

The idea that women are more conservative than men, in language as in other spheres, is a recurrent piece of folklore. It is used as an explanation when it fits, and conveniently forgotten when it does not. So on one hand, Otto Jespersen asserts that women's conservatism and modesty prevent them from innovating in language, whereas he praises men for coining 'new, fresh expressions' (1922: 247); on the other hand, in the eighteenth century at the height of the struggle to 'fix' the language, women were blamed for introducing new and ephemeral items into the English lexicon. Men, by implication more conservative, zealously guarded the purity of the standard language. It appears women are said to be conservative only when this attribute is out of favour.[2]

Trudgill (1974b: 90) quotes the examples of Koasati and Chukchi as cases where women's language preserves older forms, i.e. is more conservative than men's, implying that this is a widespread pattern. But to rely on women's conservatism as an explanation of sex differences is dangerous, as a cursory examination of Pop's comprehensive account of dialect surveys around the world (Pop 1950) will reveal: the evidence is contradictory. Many dialectologists, including Jaberg and Jud, and Pop himself, claim that women's speech *is* more conservative and therefore choose women as informants. Others, in particular Gilliéron in France and Orton in England, describe women as poor informants because they are *not* conservative. Such discrepancies require explanation themselves. Perhaps conservatism is chiefly in the mind of the researcher (and note that dialectologists were men, as were most of their fieldworkers).

There is a particular problem with the 'conservatism' explanation being applied to the findings of urban sociolinguistics. Women's speech has repeatedly been found to be closer to the prestige standard than men's; but while this could indicate conservatism on the part of middle-class women, among working-class women it would indicate the opposite. For such women, the standard variety represents innovation: a conservative pattern would involve preserving vernacular variants. The notion of conservatism is therefore unable to do what researchers have usually wanted it to do, namely explain the behaviour of women as a group.

There is, furthermore, a considerable body of evidence from sociolinguistic surveys that women *are* often in the vanguard of linguistic change. Labov (1972a: 301ff) discusses their innovative role, and his remarks receive support from subsequent studies like the Milroys' in Belfast and Romaine's in Edinburgh. Women are implicated in change particularly when it is in the direction of the prestige standard: this leads to a new explanation, replacing conservatism (which is clearly inadequate) with **status consciousness** on the part of women.

3. Status

The status explanation of linguistic sex differences is very much tied up with an approach to variation based on social stratification (Labov 1972a; Trudgill 1974a). This approach seeks to demonstrate that the distribution of variants in a speech community is socially stratified, and that some variants also have a patterned distribution that correlates with the formality of the situation in which they are uttered.

Surveys using this approach have produced the result that women have higher scores than men for prestige variants and correspondingly lower scores for vernacular variants. But women also show more marked patterns of styleshift. This gives the lie to any notion of conservatism, and leads to a belief that women may be trying to gain status through their speech patterns. This is sometimes expressed in the idea that women's speech is **hyper-correct** – an idea that fits in well with prevalent stereotypes of women as a group.

Trudgill, for instance, speculates that women may be generally more status conscious than men, both because society sets higher standards for female behaviour (all women are expected to act like 'ladies') and because women's lifestyle (by which Trudgill means domestic labour and a focus on family rather than waged work) confers little status in itself (Trudgill 1974b: 94).[3] Women are thus under pressure to acquire status by other means, such as their speech patterns. Their sensitivity to linguistic norms is associated with the insecurity of their social position.

This insecurity on the part of women offers a parallel with the insecurity of the lower middle class, who provide the classic example of hypercorrect linguistic behaviour (whereby in formal styles their scores on certain variables are nearer to the prestige standard than the scores of the highest status group, indicating conscious overcompensation). But what exactly is the relationship between the hypercorrect behaviour of lower-middle-class speakers and the behaviour of women?

An example may help to clarify this issue. Let us therefore consider the case of the glottal stop in Glasgow speech using data from Macaulay's study (1977). The glottal stop is an overtly stigmatised variant in Glasgow, and Macaulay found its use showed very clear social stratification. The biggest contrast in group scores was that between lower-middle-class men and lower-middle-class women: the female informants used 40 per cent fewer instances of glottal stop. One lower-middle-class woman used fewer glottal stops than *any* upper-middle-class informant – a finding which conforms to the classic definition of hypercorrect behaviour.

What this shows is that hypercorrection for this variable and this speech community is a pattern associated primarily with lower-middle-class *women*, rather than the lower middle class in general. There is some evidence to suggest that this is not an unusual finding: where a hypercorrect pattern is found for the second highest status group in a sample there may also be a sex

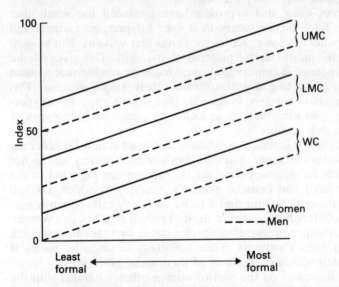

FIG. 2.1 A diagrammatic representation of stratification according to social class and sex

difference, with women exemplifying the pattern more clearly than men.[4] But even if this regularity turned out to be invariable, it would hardly license us to generalise and call the behaviour of *all* women hypercorrect, or to use the notion of hypercorrection to explain women's relatively more standardised speech. Stable linguistic variables do not produce the classic 'cross-over' pattern found in cases of hypercorrection; they lead to regular stratification, as in Fig. 2.1. Women use fewer stigmatised forms and more prestige forms in every class; it is no more justified to class this pattern of female usage hypercorrect than it would be to call the usage of the middle class hypercorrect in relation to that of the working class. The notion of women's sensitivity to prestige norms is an explanation that arises from the *intrinsic maleness of the norms*. Men's behaviour is seen as normal; when women's differs, it has to be explained.

This leads us to another matter needing explanation. If women's speech is closer to the standard, while men use more stigmatised forms, why are men not perceived as inferior speakers? The answer, according to a number of linguists, is that stigmatised variants and nonstandard varieties possess **covert prestige**. To explain the survival of stigmatised nonstandard varieties we must hypothesise a set of vernacular norms in opposition to the prescriptive and pedagogical norms with which we are all familiar. It is these vernacular norms which have prestige for working-class speakers, and which therefore exert a powerful influence on their linguistic behaviour.

In a well known paper, Trudgill (1972) linked the notion of covert prestige to the sex differences he observed in his Norwich survey. He argued that nonstandard language is associated with working-class culture and has connotations of masculinity. Thus men of all classes are more influenced by vernacular norms than women, and produce more vernacular variants.

This explanation raises problems of its own. *Why* should the vernacular be associated with masculinity? There is a strong implication here that working-class women are *outside working-class culture*: whereas men have in-group (vernacular) norms, women are perpetual 'lames' deferring to the norms of the superordinate class. Once again, men are the standard from which women can only deviate: the possibility of norms which are sex- and class-specific is not entertained. Working-class 'vernacular' culture and male culture are assumed to be one and the same thing. We will return to this point below.

There is one further problem with status-based approaches, however, that is essentially methodological, and poses the question whether the finding we are concerned with – women's greater closeness to the prestige standard – is not an artefact of the methods used to assign informants to social classes.

Both Labov and Trudgill use a standard sociological model which places heavy emphasis on occupation as an indicator of social class. But this model – on which sex-difference findings depend – itself uses sex differentiated criteria. Men are rated on their own occupations, but women are classed with the men on whom they are assumed to be dependent.

For a detailed and representative example we may take Trudgill's survey of Norwich English (Trudgill 1974a). Six criteria are used to determine social class: occupation, father's occupation, income, education, housing and locality of residence. Women informants are, however, rated on their father's occupation if single, and their husband's if married or widowed. The underlying assumption, as Trudgill himself points out, is that the whole family takes its position from the status of the father, who is assumed to be the main breadwinner. This latter assumption is by no means obvious in a society where male unemployment is widespread, and where divorce often results in single-parent families headed by women. Furthermore, Trudgill is prepared to ignore it in certain cases: he classifies married women by their own occupations if these outrank the husband's job on the Registrar-General's scale.

The inconsistencies and absurdities of stratification studies in relation to women are well documented (for an incisive critique see Delphy 1981). For our present purposes it is sufficient to point out that two factors especially relevant to people's speech patterns are their level of education and their social aspirations. In these attributes daughters need not resemble their fathers, nor wives their husbands.[5] By giving so much weight to men's occupations when classifying women, researchers give men and women within a family a parity of status that may be spurious in presicely the terms that are most important linguistically; but if this parity has to be qualified, so does the finding of clear-cut sex differences in every social class.

Are there more revealing and less sexist social indices linguists could use? There is at least one study (Douglas-Cowie 1978) which finds social ambition a better predictor than occupation, or even education, of linguistic behaviour. After getting informants in a rural Northern Irish community to rate one another for ambition, and comparing the results with scores obtained on several linguistic variables, Douglas-Cowie concluded that, except when an individual has received an unusually high level of education (e.g. has been to university), linguistic behaviour is 'clearly related to social ambition rather than . . . social status in traditional terms' (Douglas-Cowie 1978: 49).[6]

It would be interesting to see whether a social ambition measure applied to all individuals would produce significant sex differences (indeed this might serve as a test of the hypothesis that women are more status-conscious than men). It would also be important to determine the effects of age: for it Trudgill is correct in supposing that women use speech to gain status because of double standards and limited opportunities, recent social changes (altered attitudes to women and widespread unemployment among young people of both sexes) should be narrowing the gap between young women and men.[7]

Whatever the solution, it can hardly be denied that there is a problem for sociolinguistics in using the traditional model which takes the family as the primary unit of social stratification at a time when our traditional concept of the family (man in waged work, dependent unwaged wife and their children, all living in a single household) is breaking down.

4. Solidarity

Lesley Milroy (1980: 194ff) questions whether status-based models are adequate to deal with the language patterns of urban populations such as Belfast. She asserts the importance of **solidarity** as a factor influencing language use. The concept of **social network**, by enabling us to see the individual in relation to the group, refines our understanding of linguistic variation. The evidence is that a tight-knit network is an important mechanism of language maintenance. The close-knit networks to which working-class men have traditionally belonged serve to maintain vernacular norms.

Does this mean women's speech is closer to the standard than men's because women belong to weaker networks which are less efficient at enforcing linguistic norms? In Belfast, speakers from the Hammer with looser-knit networks resulting from unemployment and rehousing are not more standardised: their speech shows a drift away from the focussed vernacular norms of tighter-knit groups, but not a drift towards the prestige norms of standard English. Milroy argues that sex differences can be explained by the controlling influence of the network: men's tighter-knit networks maintain vernacular norms, whereas women's relatively looser-knit networks have less capacity to enforce focussed linguistic norms. Note the contrast between this and the status explanation, which claims women are sensitive to prestige norms. Here it is *men* who manifest sensitivity to *vernacular* norms. Women's speech is less vernacular rather than more standard.

Solidarity models seem to us to have great explanatory potential, but we want to draw attention to some problems with the social network concept as presently defined in relation to women. Two key notions which need to be examined are those of **density** and **multiplexity**. The finding that Belfast men generally have closer-knit networks than women is underpinned by the calculation of a **network strength score** for each informant; the scores (which tend to be higher for male informants) are based on five criteria, one related to density and the rest to multiplexity.

Density
The first condition an informant must satisfy to score a network strength point is (1) membership of 'a high-density, territorially based cluster' (Milroy 1980: 141). A cluster is defined as 'a portion of a personal network where relationships are denser internally than externally'. Milroy gives as examples the adolescent gangs studied by Labov, the groups formed by many young Belfast men, and middle-aged Belfast women who 'belong to clusters of six or seven individuals who meet frequently to drink tea, play cards and chat' (1980: 142). All the groups in this list are single-sex, as are the three peer groups studied by Jenny Cheshire (1982). It it always the case that dense clusters are single-sex? And if not, what are the linguistic correlates of mixed-sex clusters?

Multiplexity
Where density refers to the reciprocal links among a group of people, multiplexity refers to the different kinds of link between members of a network (for instance, they may know each other as relatives, friends, workmates, neighbours and so on). If two individuals are linked in more than one way, the link is multiplex.

Milroy's four multiplexity-related criteria for network strength are: (2) having substantial ties of kinship in the neighbourhood (more than one household in addition to his (sic) own nuclear family); (3) working in the same place as at least two others from the same area; (4) having the same place of work as at least two others of the same sex from the same area;[8] (5) voluntary association with workmates in leisure hours. The third, fourth and fifth of these conditions are male-oriented (number five in two different ways, since women's relation to 'leisure time' is different from men's; women have less of it, and are less free as to how they spend it). They are male-oriented because they relate specifically to the domain of waged work. Of course women do participate in waged work, especially in working-class communities like those Milroy studied. But they also have domestic responsibilities which these network strength criteria do not recognise.

Does this matter? Milroy herself anticipates any criticism to the effect that men will tend to score higher on the network strength scale, saying (1980: 142):

> Readers may assume that multiplex ties of the kind reflected in conditions three, four and five are usually contracted by men, and that men would, therefore, automatically score higher on the network strength scale. In fact, since both the Hammer and the Clonard are areas of high *male* unemployment, individual women frequently score as high as, or higher than men.

This observation, while perfectly true, fails to acknowledge the bias inherent in the conditions. The fact that some Hammer and Clonard women get high scores only tells us that in these areas women have taken on a 'male' role. Our criticism is that there are no parallel criteria which recognise the conditions of women's lives, and which permit points to be scored for multiplex links of a female kind (what kind is that? we beg the question deliberately). Women and men differ in their speech patterns, that is agreed; but a scoring system that throws the differences into relief by giving women low scores unless they take on male roles may be skewing our understanding of sex-linked speech patterns. We need a model of **difference** and not **deficit**.

This brings us back to a point we have already touched on: the assumption that women are outside working-class culture, or at best peripheral to it. Within the status-based approach, it will be recalled, working-class women's marginality to what is defined as the subculture (e.g. male 'street' culture in Labov's work on Black English Vernacular) is matched linguistically by a failure to use the vernacular consistently. This is explained in terms of women's allegiance to prestige rather than vernacular norms. But if we take a solidarity-based view instead, the picture is rather different. It we define vernacular norms as features which mark a speaker's loyalty to a particular network, it appears women *do* have some loyalty to vernacular norms.[9] It also appears, however, that women's identification with vernacular culture is not always marked by the same linguistic features that mark men's identification with vernacular culture.

This is clearly shown in Jenny Cheshire's study of adolescents in Reading (Cheshire 1982). Cheshire found variants which functioned differently for male and female peer groups. When the use of these variants was correlated with the individual's degree of adherence to peer group values, boys' adherence correlated with one set of variants (nonstandard *was, never* and present tense *-s*) while girls' adherence correlated with a different set (past tense *come* and *aint* as a copula).[10]

As Margaret Deuchar points out in a review (1983) 'This challenges the Labovian assumption that the social factors affecting language operate independently of one another.' The social network approach has produced a methodology which can take account of sex and class differences simultaneously, instead of abstracting them away from each other and ultimately explaining them as if 'women' and 'working class' were completely separate categories.

But findings such as Cheshire's which have emerged from this methodology give little support to the solidarity explanation of why women's speech is more standard than men's (i.e. that female networks lack the ability of male ones to enforce focussed vernacular norms). Clearly the Reading girls' group did produce shared, and distinctively *female*, norms for expressing values in opposition to the dominant values of the larger society.

5. Market forces

It is clear from the studies we have cited above that women do not always and everywhere produce speech nearer to the prestige standard than men's. Milroy's young Clonard women, for instance, maintained vernacular norms on some variables to a greater extent than their male contemporaries, and this pattern has also been found elsewhere (see Russell 1982; Thomas, Ch. 5). While social network structure is an important factor in explaining these apparent exceptions to the rule – or more neutrally, the fact that some groups of women maintain vernacular norms while others do not – it seems there is one further factor that needs to be taken into account: the differing economic opportunities open to women and men in specific speech communities. In her work on the changing speech of South Carolina, Patricia Nichols (1983) draws attention to the importance of these 'market forces'.

Nichols carried out fieldwork in two Black communities in South Carolina, paying particular attention to the effects of socioeconomic changes in precipitating a shift from the use of a low-prestige variety (Gullah) towards standard English. She found that the women in her sample did not behave uniformly.

Older mainland women were the heaviest users of Gullah variants, scoring higher on these than their male contemporaries, but younger island women, in complete contrast, were the most advanced in the shift to standard English.

Nichols explains this finding in terms of the local labour market. She suggests that certain jobs encourage or even require workers to use standard English whereas in other jobs no emphasis is placed on 'good speech'. Like most labour markets, that of the area Nichols studied is sex-segregated: men of all ages work in the construction industry, while older women work in the domestic and agricultural jobs to which Black women have until recently been confined. None of these groups has much incentive to use standard English, and the older women in particular have little opportunity even to encounter standard English speakers: they are firmly located in their own local communities. Hence the high scores of older women on Gullah variants; they, and to a slightly lesser extent the men of the community, have no reason not to maintain their vernacular.

What about the younger women who are shifting towards the standard variety? Nichols observes that new employment opportunities have opened up for these women in white collar and service jobs. Such jobs do require standard English and bring workers into contact with people who speak it, giving the young Black women both incentive and opportunity to acquire the new variety.

Nichols claims that in the South Carolina Black community, labour market forces are the single most important factor influencing linguistic choices.[11] Because the labour market is divided along gender lines, striking sex differences in language use are produced. But Nichols stresses that these particular conditions and differences cannot be generalised to every speech community. All women have in common their subordinate status relative to men, but the conditions of their lives, especially their economic position, can take many different forms depending on class, race, locality and so on. There is a crucial point here for all those who seek to explain the linguistic behaviour of women: women are not a homogeneous group, they do not always and everywhere behave in similar ways and their behaviour cannot be explained in global, undifferentiated terms.

6. Conclusion

The problems we have raised in relation to linguistic sex difference findings are of two kinds. First, we have criticised the

sociological component of sociolinguistic metholology, arguing
that sociolinguists have often been insufficiently aware of the
specific conditions of women's lives. Too little attention has been
paid to the place of women in economic and social organisation;
too little is known about the nature and values of women's
subcultures, and often this has led to an assumption that 'vernacular culture' is a uniform and exclusively masculine phenomenon.
Another serious methodological problem for correlational
approaches lies in the traditional model of social class membership which has been widely criticised for its unsatisfactory treatment of women.

Secondly, we have tried to show that the three explanations
most commonly put forward to account for sex-difference findings are inadequate, as well as being implicitly sexist (for
instance, in their tendency to attribute particular psychological
dispositions, like 'conservatism', to women as a group). The
inadequacies we have discussed have serious implications for
theoretical concepts such as 'vernacular' (how far can we maintain a notion of the vernacular as a relatively homogeneous
class/regional variety?) and 'speech community' (given differing
vernacular norms for the two scxcs, what happens to the definition of the speech community as a group with shared linguistic
norms?).

As always, there is a need for more empirical research. But
this must not be done in a framework which assumes that male
behaviour and male norms are prototypical. Explaining sex
differences does not just mean explaining the usage of women,
after all. It means devising methods applicable to all informants,
so we can gauge the importance of sex in the complex system of
intersecting social relations that supports linguistic variation.

Notes

1. The original version of this chapter was delivered to the Fifth
   Sociolinguistic Symposium held in Liverpool in 1984, and a revised
   version was published in *Language and Communication*, vol. 5,
   no. 3 (1985). The present version incorporates minor amendments
   and several additions. We are grateful to all those who have made
   comments on the paper at various stages in its evolution, and
   particularly to Lesley Milroy, to whose criticisms we have tried to
   respond. All remaining errors and shortcomings are, of course, our
   responsibility.
2. The contradiction between Jespersen's views and those of the eight-
   eenth-century purists exemplifies a tendency to identify whatever is
   thought healthy and vital with the linguistic behaviour of *men*, and

whatever is disapproved with that of *women*. A striking example from sociolinguistics itself is Labov's work on Black English Vernacular, where he writes approvingly of the vernacular as 'the mainstream in the history of the language' (1972b: 258ff) while linking it to a street culture in which women not only do not, but cannot and should not participate (1972b: 254).

3. The reason we chose to consider Trudgill's speculations in detail reflects the fact that they have been extremely influential; many people take it as read that the status explanation is true. We believe, in contrast, that it must remain speculative until more compelling evidence is adduced for women's greater status consciousness.

4. Cf. Newbrook's study of the Wirral (1983), which found a variant considered 'hypercorrect' to be favoured by women to a greater extent than men. Newbrook, however, did not subdivide his sample for social class, so it is hard to say if the pattern he uncovered was the same as the Glasgow pattern or not.

5. According to Marie Haug (1973), working-class women in the USA are likely to have a higher level of education than their husbands. In Haug's study of working couples using census data collected in 1970, this was the case for more than 50 per cent of young and middle-aged working-class women.

6. Douglas-Cowie's methods appear to work less well in studies where the investigator is an outsider to the community, and this suggests they would raise severe problems in large-scale surveys (Milroy, personal communication). Even so, it should not be beyond our wit to find some way of incorporating social ambition as a nonlinguistic variable.

7. We are aware of one study that suggests this is happening: Ulseth's 'Stress and toneme as used by Trondheim speakers: a sociolinguistic study', cited by Chambers and Trudgill (1980: 100).

8. Since (4) specifies same-sex links, two out of the five network-strength conditions value same-sex rather than mixed-sex links. It is in fact built into network theory that high levels of social segregation of the sexes occur where networks are strongest.

9. Features that act as markers of group identity are those which have a high correlation with the nonlinguistic variable measuring degree of integration into a group (e.g. 'network strength score' or 'adherence to vernacular culture'). But this does not necessarily imply that the linguistic variant concerned has a high frequency of overall use, as would be the case with vernacular variants in the Labovian paradigm. Indeed, it would be possible for a group that attached *no* significance to feature x to use it more than a group for which it was a marker of identity. Our thanks to Lesley Milroy for clarifying this important point.

10. Cheshire defines vernacular culture using male-oriented criteria like fighting and stealing which fit the girls less well. No attempt is made to discover forms of tabooed behaviour that are meaningful for girls (e.g. degrees of sexual activity).

11. Nichols (1983) acknowledges the utility of social network structure
    in explaining these choices. But this is not incompatible with empha-
    sising economic relations, since 'market forces' and employment
    patterns are important determinants of a person's social network
    structure.

Chapter 3

A pragmatic account of women's use of standard speech[1]

Margaret Deuchar

1. Introduction

Several sociolinguistic studies (e.g. Labov 1966; Trudgill 1974a;
Milroy 1980) have found that in western, industrial societies,
women tend to produce speech closer to the standard in pronunciation than that of men. The main explanations advanced for
this phenomenon are in terms of sociological factors external to
language such as status consciousness or solidarity. I shall show
that neither of these explanations is entirely satisfactory, but that
the phenomenon can be explained in terms of pragmatic, interactional notions internal to language use. The notions I shall
make use of are those of face and power as used by Brown and
Levinson (1978) in their model of politeness.

2. Findings to be explained

To begin with we must be clear about what is meant by the
finding that women produce speech closer to the standard than
that of men. This finding is based mainly on work done in the
USA and Britain, but also in other western, industrialised countries. What the studies have in common is that they are
conducted in places where there is a recognised standard pronunciation, such as Received Pronunciation in Britain, and they are
based on data collected in a variety of situations, ranging from
interviews to informal conversations. The speech data are coded
for particular variables, and scored in terms of a scale which
reflects how close their variants are to standard pronunciation.
So for example, in Trudgill's (1974) study of the variable (ng),
i.e. the pronunciation of the suffix in verbs like *walking*,

laughing, a score of 1 was assigned for each instance of [ɪŋ], and 2 for each instance of [ɪn]. Since [ɪŋ] is the standard pronunciation, the lower an individual's mean score, the closer their speech is considered to be to the standard, whereas the higher the score, the further away. On average Trudgill found that women scored lower than men, indicating that their pronunciation was closer to the standard than that of men. In order to explain this and other findings of the same kind, various explanations have been put forward. Two of these, as Cameron and Coates point out in Chapter 2, are in terms of status consciousness and solidarity.

3. Explanation A: Status consciousness

The status consciousness explanation is put forward by Trudgill (1983), who cites what he calls the sociological 'finding' that women are more status-conscious then men. He suggests that as women have lower social status than men they are more aware of the value of linguistic indicators of status. He also suggests that women are traditionally rated on how they appear rather than on what they do, and that pronunciation is subsumed under appearance. There is a problem, however, about the assumption that women actually are more status-conscious than men. Trudgill's source for this assumption is Martin (1954), who showed that women were more likely than men to claim membership of the middle class when the researcher assigned them to the working class. But since the researcher in Martin's study classified women mostly on the basis of their husbands' or fathers' social class, whereas men were classified on their own terms, it is perhaps not surprising that women were more likely than men to disagree with the researcher's classification. So we are left in doubt about whether women are really more status-conscious than men. Even if they are, however, we need to ask why they should use linguistic markers of status which neither reflect nor determine their real status.

4. Explanation B: Solidarity

If we now turn to the solidarity explanation of women's use of standard speech, we can identify two versions, that of Trudgill (1974a) and that of Milroy (1980). Trudgill attempts to account for the converse of women's use of standard speech, i.e. men's greater use of nonstandard speech, in terms of what we may call masculine solidarity. Trudgill's work on self-evaluation shows that men appear to value nonstandard speech more than women, and he suggests that nonstandard speech may have a covert prestige associated with masculinity. The only problem is an unexplained anomaly in his study: women under 30 seem to attach the same covert prestige to nonstandard speech. Assuming that the women in this age group still produce relatively more standard speech than men (and we are not given the data) we lose sight of a neat relationship between evaluation of language, sex and linguistic behaviour.

Milroy's solidarity explanation is based on what we may call network solidarity. She suggests that vernacular (i.e. nonstandard) speech is likely to be maintained to a greater extent in dense, multiplex networks than in looser networks, and her study shows that men have higher network scores, based on density and multiplexity, than women. However, as Cameron and Coates point out in Chapter 2, most of the criteria for multiplexity are oriented towards a typically male life-style, assuming participation in paid employment and a clear separation between work and leisure. So the higher network scores of men may be an artefact of the methodology, and are anyway at odds with suggestions by others (Brown 1980; Nichols 1984; Thomas, Ch. 5) that women working at home tend to participate in denser and more multiplex networks than those working outside the home.

5. Explanation C: Face and power

All the explanations of women's speech that we have discussed so far have been in terms of factors external to the process of communication, and all have been found wanting in some respect. I want to suggest now that Brown and Levinson's model of politeness points the way towards an explanation involving notions which are basic to the way language is used for communicative purposes. The key notions, as in the politeness model, are those of face and of power.

Brown and Levinson (1978: 66) define the notion of face as 'the public self-image that every member wants to claim for himself'. This consists of two aspects, negative face and positive face. Negative face involves the desire for freedom of action and freedom from imposition, while positive face involves the desire for approval. Power, or 'P' is defined as 'an asymmetric social dimension of relative power' (p. 82). This means that in an interaction, the speaker can be characterised as relatively more or less powerful than the addressee.

In order to use the notions of face and power to explain women's greater use of standard speech we need four assumptions:

1. participants in an interaction wish to protect their own face;
2. attention to other's face is affected by relative power in relation to other;
3. attention to other's face may involve damage to one's own;
4. women have less relative power than men.

Assumptions (1), (2) and (3) are derived from Brown and Levinson's politeness model, while (4) is my own.

The first assumption is derived by Brown and Levinson from the work of Goffman (1967). Brown and Levinson do not deal with all aspects of face maintenance, but concentrate on those which give rise to politeness strategies. This means that they deal mainly with attention by the speaker to the addressee's face when the speaker is performing what they call a face threatening act. To give an example, a request by a speaker to borrow money can be seen as a potentially face threatening act, since it may offend an addressee's negative face, or their desire not to be imposed on. A speaker can mitigate the potential threat, however, by prefacing the request with an apology for bothering the addressee. The apology is a politeness strategy which has the effect of paying attention to the addressee's negative face.

In Brown and Levinson's model, whether or not attention is actually paid to face depends on various factors, which include the relative power of the speaker and addressee. The more powerful is the addressee in relation to the speaker, the more likely it is that the speaker will pay attention to the addressee's face, and the less likely it is that the speaker's own face will receive attention from the addressee. So a relatively powerless speaker would probably pay attention to the addressee's face by politeness when making a request to borrow money, but might not obtain the same attention when receiving the request. So relatively powerless participants in an interaction will receive relatively little attention to their own faces.

Furthermore, because such powerless speakers regularly pay attention to the face of others by politeness strategies, they may actively cause damage to their own faces. This follows from assumption (3), that attention to another's face may involve damage to one's own. This is based on the fact that many of the strategies of politeness cause damage to the speaker's own face while protecting that of the addressee. In using the strategies of positive politeness listed by Brown and Levinson (1978: 107), a speaker is likely to damage his or her own negative face. For example, a promise to perform a service pays attention to the addressee's positive face, but threatens the negative face of the speaker in so far as it is an imposition on his or her freedom of action. Conversely, strategies of negative politeness (see Brown and Levinson 1978: 136) tend to threaten the speaker's own positive face. This can be illustrated with the example of the apology given earlier. While an apology pays attention to the negative face of the addressee by acknowledging a potential imposition, it threatens the speaker's own positive face by admitting a transgression.

Assuming that women are relatively powerless speakers (assumption (4)), then they will receive little attention to their own faces, and will damage their own while paying attention to the face of others. Yet we assume that they have face wants like anyone else (assumption (1)). So how can their own faces be protected in ways which do not threaten the face of others? Just as attention to the face of another may damage one's own face, so attention to one's own face may threaten that of another. To take an example, boasting would protect the speaker's own face, but implicitly threaten that of the addressee by indirectly belittling him or her.

However, the use of standard speech, with its connotations of prestige, appears suitable for protecting the face of a relatively powerless speaker without attacking that of the addressee. It could only be conceived of as threatening the addressee's face if it involved what Giles (1973) calls 'accent divergence' from the less standard speech of the addressee. But this kind of strategy would be typical of the powerful rather than the powerless. Giles describes accent divergence as involving the exaggeration of pronunciation differences betweeen oneself and one's addressee so as to dissociate oneself from them (which could be seen as a threat to their positive face). Divergence for a given speaker can involve either an 'upward' movement towards the standard, or a 'downward' movement away from the standard. Upward accent divergence would occur with an addressee speaking a nonstandard variety, and thus very likely having less power than the speaker. It would thus only be used by women in relatively powerful positions. A strategy quite likely to be used by women and powerless people, however, is upward accent convergence, described by Giles (1973: 90) as follows:

if a sender in social interaction perceives the pronunciation patterns of his receiver as relatively higher in terms of accent prestige than his own idiolect, provided that his intentions and social desires are those of integration and gaining approval, the modification of his accent towards that of his receiver may be termed 'upward accent convergence'.

In terms of face, this could be seen as a strategy of positive politeness in so far as it pays attention to the positive face of the addressee. It also protects the speaker's face, however, because of the prestige of the standard. So when women use standard speech, they are protecting their own faces, and are sometimes paying attention to the face of the addressee at the same time, but would rarely be threatening it.

I have tried to show in this paper that previous explanations of women's greater use of standard speech in terms of factors external to language use are unsatisfactory. However, it is possible to account for this important sociolinguistic finding in terms of notions which are basic to the process of interaction. Assuming women have face wants to the same extent as men, and yet less relative power, the use of standard speech is a way of maintaining their own face without threatening that of the addressee.

Note

1. This chapter was originally presented as a paper at the International Pragmatics Conference, Viareggio, Italy, September 1985.

Chapter 4

The speech of British Black women in Dudley, West Midlands[1]

Viv Edwards

1. Introduction

Until recently the history of the study of Black speech in Britain has been one of neglect and has thus closely paralleled the study of Black speech in other parts of the world. The present paper is based on the speech of the children and grandchildren of Jamaicans who first started to settle in Britain in the mid-1950s and now live in Dudley, West Midlands. The study of which it is a part represents the first major sociolinguistic investigation of British Black speech. Previous discussions of Black language in Britain have tended to rely heavily on anecdotal accounts and self-reports. In contrast, the Dudley study is based on an actual corpus of data which draws on the speech of a wide range of young British Blacks in a wide range of situations.

While the Dudley study draws on the speech of both young men and young women, the focus of the present paper is the speech of the female participants in the study. The overall findings of our analysis do not indicate that sex has a statistically significant effect on the language behaviour of British Black people. None the less, I will argue that the variable of sex needs to be considered very carefully in relation to research design, sampling methodology and interpretation of results. Finally, I will discuss the way in which the stereotypical picture of the Patois speaker as the angry male underachiever is seriously challenged both by our findings as a whole and by considering a case study of one of the young women who took part in the study.

2. The study of Black language: an historical perspective

The study of Black speech in Britain and elsewhere has a surprisingly long and interesting history, though this has been submerged. Civil servants were expected to acquire a rudimentary knowledge of the language spoken in the subject nations which they were going to administer, and languages such as Hausa, Kiswahili, Persian, Urdu and Arabic have been studied in British universities and select schools since the beginning of the century (Alladina 1986).

In areas such as the Caribbean and America, however, where there was a larger population of white settlers and black people had been forcibly transported as slaves, there were no such pragmatic considerations. Plantation owners deliberately operated a 'divide and rule' policy, by mixing slaves from different parts of Africa whose languages were not mutually intelligible. The only Africans with any degree of contact with Europeans were the freedmen and artisans, and documents from this period show that these particular individuals spoke good, easily intelligible English (Alleyne 1971).

The main concern for the majority of the slave population, however, was to develop a common means of communication with one another. In territories where English was the language of the white settlers, pidgins emerged which drew predominantly on English as their vocabulary base. In French-dominated territories, the vocabulary base was French. As the pidgins became the first language of subsequent generations of slaves, they gradually underwent a process of creolisation. Today, continuing contact with English through school, government and the media has produced what writers such as De Camp (1971) refer to as a post-creole continuum. Caribbean varieties of creole speech remain further removed from English than Black American speech, though many similarities are still to be found between the speech of Black people throughout the Americas and the Caribbean.

Attitudes towards distinctively Black speech have tended to be extremely antipathetic. Herskovitz (1937), for instance, reports that until the late 1930s, the most common hypothesis put forward to explain Negro speech was that it was 'the blind groping of minds too primitive in modes of speech beyond their capabilities'. And young linguists were advised not to jeopardise their careers by studying 'marginal languages' (Hymes 1971). It was not until the 1960s that linguists such as Bailey and Labov turned their attention to the description of Black speech in both the Caribbean and the USA and began to realise the central importance of creole speech communities for linguistic theory.

It is notable, however, that when the spotlight was finally turned on Black speech, a disproportionate amount of attention was placed on the speech of Black males. Labov *et. al.*'s (1968) study of peer group speech was based exclusively on recordings of male adolescents. His subsequent description of ritual insult (Labov 1972c) draws on the performances of this same group and presents this speech event as an exclusively male activity. Abrahams (1972a, 1972b) provides a rich and wide-ranging description of speech events in the Caribbean. However, the titles of his articles – 'The training of the man of words in talking sweet' and 'The training of the man of words in talking broad' – reflect a similar preoccupation with male speakers.

Those reading accounts of Black speech communities in the 1960s and 1970s could be forgiven for assuming that only the male members of those communities were linguistically adept and talented performers in socially prized speech events. The failure to discuss or describe the speech of the Black women could only serve to reinforce stereotypes of passivity and submission. An alternative and very different view, however, emerges from even the briefest survey of literary history. While linguists describe speech events such as 'Playing the Dozens', an exercise in ritual insult, as an exclusively male activity, writers like Brown (1969) and Ladner (1972), refer in their work to girls who were extremely skilled players. The distortion which seems to have occurred in the linguistic literature can no doubt be explained in terms of the androcentrism of society as a whole. It is also possible to look at what happened in terms of errors of omission: since most linguists were male, they would have easiest access to male speakers. They would not necessarily have made the same errors of omission had they been black and members of the same speech community as that which they were describing.

3. Black speech in Britain

The post-war boom economy created a serious labour shortage in Britain. Large employers such as London Transport and the National Health Service took the unprecedented step of launching advertising campaigns to attract new workers in New Commonwealth countries, including the former British West Indies. There had been a long history of migration from the Caribbean, but the traditional destination, the USA, had become inaccessible as a result of the 1952 McCarran Act. Britain became the new focus for migration. By 1971, the West Indian population in Britain was estimated at 543,000, just over 1 per cent of the total population. Increasingly stringent immigration legislation enacted during the 1960s, however, meant that by the end of the decade new arrivals had come to a virtual standstill. Since the mid-1970s almost all Black children entering school have been born in Britain.

The study of Black speech in Britain has been one of the same kind of neglect documented for the Caribbean and America. Despite the presence of large numbers of West Indians from the mid-1950s onwards, the first serious academic study of their speech, Wells's description of the phonological adaptation of Jamaicans in London, did not appear until 1973. Only one other major publication on Black British speech – Edwards (1979) – appeared during this decade, though the 1980s have finally seen a burgeoning of interest in this area (Sutcliffe 1982; Le Page & Tabouret-Keller 1985; Dalphinis 1985; Sebba 1986; Edwards 1986; Sutcliffe & Wong 1986).

A similar history of neglect can be detected in the funding of research into Black speech. The Concept 7–9 curriculum project on the language of West Indian children was not set up until 1967, despite the presence of Black children in British school during the 10 previous years. The first descriptive research projects to be funded were undertaken in the 1980s and received between them a budget of only £70,000. There has been further criticism (cf. Alladina 1986) that all those in receipt of awards were white and outsiders to the community they were describing.

The research on British Black speech has not, however, been guilty of the same androcentric bias as is found in the research on West Indian and American Black speech communities, and empirical studies have all drawn on both male and female speech. Some interesting insights on male–female speech differences have emerged from these studies and bring into question many of the assumptions about Black speech which over the years have become conventional wisdom.

In this chapter, I want to focus on some of the sex-related issues which we encountered during a study of the language of British-born Black adolescents in Dudley in the West Midlands. The work was undertaken by white linguists working in conjunction with black fieldworkers. Great care was taken to guard against the dangers of perceiving Black speech through a white cultural matrix. The account which follows remains, never the less, the work of an outsider. Hopefully, work undertaken by Black linguists will confirm or refute these observations in the not too distant future.

4. The Dudley study

4.1 Some considerations for field work

Because the first language of British Blacks is now the local white variety, many people have concluded that Patois is a spent force, reserved only for the older generation and certain fringe elements within the Black community, such as Rastafarians. These assumptions, however, are based largely on the observations of white people, such as teachers, interacting with young Black people in formal settings such as school. The aim of the present study was to record the speech of a representative cross-section of young British Black people. In order to ensure that we were examining the full linguistic repertoires of the young people participating in the study, it was essential to collect speech from a wide range of situations differing in both formality and the racial origin of participants. The corpus of speech data collected in this way would thus enable us to confirm or refute anecdotal observations made by predominantly white observers.

Potential differences between male and female speech had important implications for the research design. In the pilot which preceded the main study, it had been assumed that the presence of a Black fieldworker would be enough to trigger Patois speech in conversations where all the participants were Black. This did not prove to be the case. At this stage the only fieldworker was Carol Tomlin, a young Black woman. She was relatively successful in eliciting Patois from the female speakers who formed part of her own social network, but markedly less so when talking with young men, particularly those she did not know prior to recording. At her suggestion, we decided to ask Leighton Bruce, a young Black man, to join the project as a second fieldworker.

For similar reasons, the young people who made up our sample were always recorded in single-sex friendship groups of two or three. In both formal and informal interactions with a Black fieldworker, it was arranged that the fieldworker should be the same sex as the friendship group. This methodology allowed us to achieve two inter-related aims. First, it made it possible to avoid any variation which might be attributable to inhibiting factors inherent in mixed-sex conversation (cf. Cameron 1985; Coates 1986). Second, because Patois usage seems to be linked in part at least to the sex of the participants in the conversation, it allowed us to record a much greater volume of Patois speech.

Some 45 British-born adolescents were recorded in the following situations: in a formal interview with a white fieldworker; in a formal interview with a Black fieldworker; in informal racially mixed conversation; alone in single-sex peer-group conversation; and in informal conversation with the Black fieldworker. The patterns of language use which emerged were found to vary with both formality and ethnicity. The validity of these findings, however, would have been considerably more limited if the variable of sex had not been carefully controlled.

4.2 Response variables and explanatory variables

Three separate language measures were used in the analysis of the recorded speech. The first was a Patois frequency score, based on the mean frequency of occurrence of some 11 commonly occurring Patois features for each speaker. The next score, the Patois competence score, focussed on how many of a list of 20 Patois features occurred at some point in recording for a given speaker. Finally a Patois pattern score indicated how many of the five situations a speaker chose to mark as Black by using Patois features (see V. Edwards 1986 for more detailed discussion of these variables).

The aim of the analysis was to determine the extent to which these response variables were related to a number of explanatory variables. The explanatory variables included sex of speaker; education (based on both actual achievements and aspirations); social network; and attitudes towards mainstream white society.

4.3 Results

Statistically significant relationships were found to hold between frequency scores and three different explanatory variables: network relations; the interaction of education and sex; and attitudes towards mainstream white society. It became clear that the more integrated the speaker into the Black community, the more frequent the use of Patois is likely to be. Similarly the more critical the attitude of the speaker towards mainstream white society, the greater the use of Patois variants. The effect of education was less clear cut. In the present sample, education appeared to decrease the frequency of Patois usage in young men, but to have no effect on the speech of young women.

The other linguistic measures, Patois competence and patterns of Patois usage, were found to correlate only with one of the explanatory variables, viz. social network. It emerged that the more integrated into the Black community, the more competent the level of Patois, and the larger the number of situations in which Patois features were used.

It might appear on the basis of these main findings that sex is not an important factor in the linguistic behaviour of speakers. Closer analysis of a number of issues, however, suggests that this interpretation of the results represents a considerable oversimplification, and that fundamental problems in sampling methodology are masking important differences between male and female speakers.

4.4 Adequacy of the sample

Any socially sensitive description of British Black language needs to draw on a sample of speakers who represent the groups and norms observed to be important within the community. Sampling methodology in a study of this kind, however, poses a number of intractable problems. The two main alternatives are to work with a random sample or to decide on the basis of prior study the meaningful divisions within the community and to draw on a smaller 'judgment' or 'quota' sample which reflects these divisions.

In studies of language two main reasons are proposed for preferring judgement samples. The first is based on the theoretical argument that, because linguistic behaviour tends to be more homogeneous than other kinds of behaviour (cf. Sankoff 1980; Milroy 1987), increased data handling brings diminishing analytical returns. The second is more practical and derives from the immense problems of working with large samples. Judgement samples can, of course, be representative only in a weak and nontechnical sense. None the less, the relationships between language and social factors which can be detected using samples of this kind can leave little doubt as to their validity.

Within a British Black context two main obstacles – the absence of a ready made sample frame and the skewed distribution of the British Black population – make a judgement sample the only possible option. Perhaps the most fundamental of these problems is the lack of sampling frame. The census, for instance, contains information on country of birth but not on language or ethnicity, and is therefore of no help in identifying British-born Black people. In the case of linguistic minority groups such as the Jews, Greek Cypriots, Sikhs and Chinese whose names give important clues as to their ethnicity, various name-analysis methods have been devised (cf. De Lange & Kosmin 1979; Leewenberg 1979; Singh 1979; Chin & Simsova 1981). The British Black community, however, cannot be identified by their names. Nor can British Black people be reliably identified from community lists, because they form too large and heterogeneous a group.

The second difficulty concerns the nonrandom distribution of the Black population. Because of the nature of immigration to Britain, the vast majority of Black people are to be found in a relatively small number of urban centres and are further concentrated in certain areas of these cities. The situation is complicated still further by the widespread discrimination which Black people in Britain experience (cf. D. Smith 1976; C. Brown 1984; Jenkins & Troyna 1983). Because Black people are artificially concentrated in the lower socioeconomic groups, social class is a poor index of values and attitudes and does not have the same predictive value as in mainstream white society.

A reliable judgement sample can only be achieved on the basis of careful ethnographic observation of both the structural norms and values, and of the areas which unite and divide individuals within that community (cf. Blom & Gumperz 1972). The present description is based on both the shared characteristics of the speakers in the sample (place of birth, parents' island of origin, age and residence) and those characteristics which differentiate speakers (sex, education, social network and attitudes towards mainstream white society).

The speakers in our sample were British-born Black people whose parents had come from Jamaica. At the time of field work they were between the ages of 16 and 23 and were living in Dudley, West Midlands. A total of 21 young women and 24 young men took part in recordings. These speakers ranged from former pupils of schools for the educationally subnormal to polytechnic students; they represented a wide range of attitudes towards white people and society; they varied in their social networks from those whose relationships were exclusively Black to those who came into regular contact with a wide range of white people.

It was, however, easier to satisfy some of these conditions than others. For instance, it was fairly straightforward to ensure approximately equal numbers of males and females, and to determine whether participants had lived all their lives in Dudley and whether their parents came from Jamaica. Various other characteristics were more difficult to determine in advance. For instance, it was only possible to discover attitudes towards mainstream white society, educational aspirations and social networks by fairly detailed questioning during the course of recording.

It emerged that the sample was remarkable for the excellent spread of scores for these variables, but was less impressive when each of these variables was broken down into male and female components. Although the number of males and females was approximately equal, the distribution of scores tended to differ between the sexes. If we consider the overall results, we are forced to conclude that sex does not exert a statistically significant effect on the speech of young Black people when considered as an independent variable. However, sex-related patterns which can be detected within each of the significant explanatory variables suggest that it would be premature to dismiss the effect of sex on the language behaviour of the British Black community.

4.5 Social Network

An analysis in terms of social network rather than social class has a number of advantages in a study of the language of British Black people in as much as it is independent of intercultural differences in economic or status systems. Social network measures a person's degree of group membership. Most rural communities and working-class communities in old established areas of cities are characterised by closed networks, where there is more contact with other members of the network than with people outside. In a closed system a great deal more social pressure can be brought to bear on members to conform to the behavioural norms of the group than in open networks which are made up of individuals who do not necessarily know one another.

The determinants of social network vary from community to community and close ethnographic observation is therefore required to determine which factors are important in a given community. Gal (1979), for instance, reports that degrees of peasantness were critical in her study of Austrian-Hungarian bilinguals. W. Edwards (1984) suggests that main differences between vernacular urban culture in Guyana can be characterised in terms of frequenting of rum shops, street dancing, preference for certain kinds of music and dress, while vernacular rural culture is associated with attendance at African derived pre-nuptial festivities, rustic dress and Afro-Guyanese cuisine.

In the present study it was felt that the most important determinants of social network were patterns of work, friendship and leisure. For instance, young people living in a predominantly Black neighbourhood and basing their social life on the Pentecostal Church would form part of a much more closed social network system than young people living in the same predominantly Black community but working mainly with white people and socialising in racially mixed groups.

Social network scores were based on answers to a wide range of questions. Speakers were asked where they lived and whether they were employed. They were also asked to name their three

closest friends, to indicate whether they were Black or white and
where they went together (for instance, youth club, work, church
or sport). Thus, if speakers went to more than one place with a
given friend it suggested that network relations were multiplex,
and if they went to the same place with more than one friend that

TABLE 4.1   Calculation of network scores

	Range
Employment	0 to 1
Residence	0 to 1
Black friends	0 to 3
Activities with black friends: dense	0 to 1
multiplex	0 to 1
Social activities	0 to 2
White friends	−1 to 1
White neighbours	−1 to 1
Total	−2 to 11

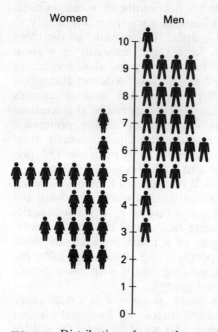

FIG. 4.1   Distribution of network scores for male and female speakers

they were dense (cf. Milroy 1980). They were also asked questions about their leisure activities. Attention was paid to whether they mentioned known Black activities such as Pentecostal Church or the local Black youth club. Level of involvement was also noted. Thus, if a speaker was a committed Christian rather than an occasional church-goer they would be involved in a wide range of extra activities such as bible class and church youth club. Finally questions were asked about the frequency with which speakers saw white friends and neighbours socially.

Actual scores varied from 2 to 10. Figure 4.1 shows that the spread between the two extremes was good over the sample as a whole, but males and females tended to pattern differently, males being more likely to have a higher network score than females.

4.6 Acquiescence–criticalness

The growing catalogue of racial inequalities in the areas of employment, education, housing and the public sector has been documented in a number of reports and surveys (cf. D. Smith 1976; A. Rampton 1981; C. Brown 1984). The British Black community, however, is by no means a single homogeneous group and it should not be surprising, therefore, that the response of Black people to racial discrimination – and how they see their own position in a predominantly white society – varies enormously.

Various writers (e.g. Giles 1977; Taylor 1980) have pointed to the centrality of language in the discussion of intergroup relations. Ethnic markers in speech can be increased in order to maximise social distance or reduced in order to minimise their difference, and are thus of fundamental importance in the modelling of social identity. Given the links between language and identity, it was important to establish the range of attitudes towards mainstream white society and to determine whether the nature and degree of any relationship which might hold between social attitudes and language behaviour.

Following on the work of Fuller (1983), a scale of acquiescence–criticalness was devised, based on speakers' opinions of three areas of inter-racial contact which are known to be particularly emotive within the Black community: school, work and the police.

● How would you describe your time at school?
  Very happy/ quite happy/OK/quite unhappy/very unhappy
● How many teachers do you think were prejudiced against Black children?

All or almost all/more than half/about half/less than half/none or very few
- What about white people as a whole?
All or almost all/more than half/about half/less than half/none or very few
- How do you think teachers found *you* as a person?
Very co-operative/quite co-operative/OK/quite difficult/very difficult
- How do you think teachers found the way you worked?
Very hard-working/quite hard-working/OK/quite lazy/very lazy
- What do you think of the way the police treat black people?
Very fair/quite fair/OK/quite unfair/very unfair
- If you were stopped and questioned by the police what would you do?
Try to get away/co-operate but complain/co-operate without complaining

Potential scores on this measure ranged from $+ 13$ to $- 13$. Actual scores varied from $+ 7$ to $- 7$. Although male and female speakers in this case achieve the same range of scores, closer examination again throws up some interesting questions for any analysis in terms of sex, in that males tend overall to be more critical than females.

4.7 Education

The extensive educational underperformance of Black children in British schools (cf. Rampton 1981; Stone 1980; Tomlinson 1984) makes any analysis of the relationship between level of educational achievement and language behaviour potentially problematic. In stark contrast with the actual performance, educational aspirations on the part of both parents and children have always tended to be high (Black Peoples' Progressive Association 1978; Tomlinson 1984). In the present study, it was

TABLE 4.2   Calculation of education scores

CSEs	passed: 2	planned: 1
O-levels	passed: 4	planned: 2
A-levels	passed: 6	planned: 3
Craft training (e.g. City and Guilds)		1
Professional training (e.g. State Registered Nurse)		2
Tertiary education (including 'Access' courses)		3

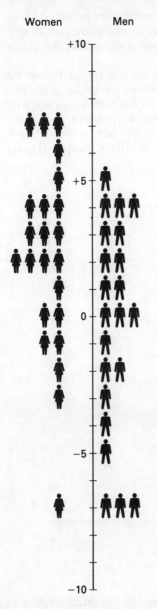

FIG. 4.2 Distribution of acquiescence–criticalness scores for male and female speakers

therefore felt to be more realistic to combine measures of actual academic achievement as measured by examination results with any future plans for training or further study which the young people in the sample might have.

Scores varied between o and 10 as we can see in Figure 4.3 which shows the distribution of education scores for male and female speakers. Again we find a good spread of scores but with a slight imbalance, the females tending to perform and aspire higher than the males. This pattern in fact reflects trends reported in the population at large for Black people (Driver 1980; Fuller 1983).

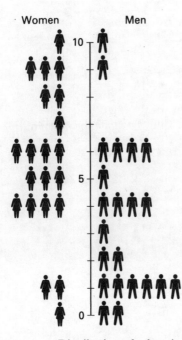

FIG. 4.3   Distribution of education scores for male and female speakers

5. Discussion

The findings of the study therefore need to be interpreted with caution. While it is clear that social network is by far the most important determinant of language behaviour, it should be remembered that the network relations of males are more closed than those of females. Higher rates of youth unemployment among males, for instance, make it likely that young men will spend a higher proportion of their time with other unemployed friends in the Black community. Higher levels of underachievement in school no doubt have a similar effect. It should also be noted that this pattern of male underachievement had an unfortunate effect on the composition of the sample, with female underachievers being poorly represented in the group as a whole. It is possible that a sample more equally balanced for educational achievement might have shown young men and women behaving in a similar way.

It is important to acknowledge the weaknesses in the sampling methodology. It is also important to recognise the strength of the arguments for interpreting with caution the effect of sex on language behaviour. None the less, the usefulness of our findings in challenging widely held stereotypes about the language of the British Black community should not be underestimated. The popular stereotype of the Patois speaker is male, underachieving and hostile to white society. The findings of the present study suggest that this view is, at the very least, a gross oversimplification. Statistically significant correlations were indeed found to hold between overall frequency of Patois features and attitudes to mainstream white society on the one hand and low educational achievement in boys on the other hand. Yet there were many examples of highly competent Patois speakers in our sample who were neither particularly hostile towards whites, nor underperforming in school. For the purposes of the present discussion, it is also important to note that many of the most competent Patois speakers were women.

Purely quantitative approaches to the study of language in society can be extremely helpful in identifying trends in the data which might not otherwise be discernible. Statistical analysis has the added advantage of being able to demonstrate whether any observed effects are due to genuine effects or merely chance fluctuations of the data. However, when we focus on the overall picture in this way we risk losing sight of the individuals on whom the study is based. In an attempt to redress this balance, I would like to end with a brief case study.

6. Polly

Polly is 18. Although she left school without taking exams, she is actively considering taking evening classes to get some recognised qualifications. She is unemployed at the moment but has done two Youth Opportunity placements in catering, each lasting six months. She is anxious to work again because, as she says, 'The days are too boring.'

Polly is not particularly radical in her thinking. For instance, unlike many of her contemporaries, she dislikes the idea of separate clubs for Blacks and whites, which she feels entails unnecessary segregation. None the less, she is very critical of both the police handling of young people and various aspects of education. She points out that when she was at school she learnt nothing about Black language and culture. She considers that Black Studies should be made widely available and taught to white pupils as well as Black. She also draws attention to the question of Black children and sport and the unfortunate implications for achievement in academic subjects of high teacher expectations of Black pupils in this area: 'Our netball team was mainly black girls. Instead of going to, say, the French lesson, we'd go and practise'. Polly's social networks are mainly Black. She sees white friends occasionally, but never visits white neighbours. She has a close circle of Black friends and their main interest is night clubbing. Although many of her friends are Christian, she is not a regular church goer.

Polly monitors out all Patois features from her speech in situations where white speakers are present. Her phonology is unmistakeably West Midlands and she also shows signs of nonstandard British English grammar. When defending Rastafarianism, for instance, she says:

> I mean like, say, with my Mum, right. She just saw some [Rastas] and said, 'Oh, he's no good', cos he'd got locks on his head.' You know Junior Palmer? I tell you, him and my Mum! When my Mum got to know him, the two of them, they were like that. Junior couldn't do nothing wrong. You know love, Junior was gold.

Polly's linguistic repertoire is by no means restricted to a West Midlands variety and in situations where the other participants are Black her use of Patois is impressive. She uses a very wide range of Patois features and her delivery is fast and fluent. She switches frequently between 'English' and 'Patois' in codeswitching behaviour reminiscent of speakers in stable bilingual communities in many parts of the world (cf. Poplack 1980). This switching may take place even within the same sentence and it often achieves dramatic or amusing effects.

> With Melanie right, you have to say she speaks *tri different sort of language when she want to. Cos she speak half Patois, half English*

and when im ready im will come out wid, 'I day and I bay and I ay this and I ay that.[2] I day have it and I day know where it is' . . . And then she goes, '*Lord God, I so hot*'. Now she'll be sitting there right and she'll go, 'It's hot, isn't it?', you know, and you think which one is he[her son] going to grow up speaking.

The picture which emerges from a close examination of Polly's speech is that she is a highly competent speaker with an extensive linguistic repertoire which she uses to some considerable effect.

7. Conclusion

If Black speech has received very little attention in the past then Black women's language has, until very recently, been totally overlooked. Yet a number of important considerations emerge on close examination of the information currently available. Our own work in Dudley, for instance, points very clearly to the importance of addressing the variable of sex in both research design and fieldwork. The full range of a speaker's linguistic repertoire is only likely to be tapped if provision is made for the recording of single-sex groups in racially homogeneous groups.

It is also important to look closely at the effect of sex on patterns of language behaviour. Although, at first sight, our findings did not support the notion that sex was a significant explanatory variable for the inter-individual differences which we noted, closer examination would support a more cautious intepretation of our results. Consider, for instance, social network – the most important of the explanatory variables. Although the spread of network scores across the sample is good for both male and female speakers, males and females tend to pattern differently, with males being more likely to have higher network scores. By the same token, males and females have a similar range of scores on measures of their attitudes to mainstream white society, but males tend, overall, to be more critical than females. Thus, while there are no statistically significant differences between the young women and the young men in the sample, it is important to note these tendencies.

It is also important to remember that, independent of statistically significant patterning which occurs in our data, there are many individuals who strongly challenge a number of common stereotypes. The Patois speaker is normally represented as male, underachieving and hostile to mainstream white society. Yet the most proficient Patois speakers included young people who had done well at school and who showed no strong hostility towards the white *status quo*. Most important for the purposes of the

present chapter, these fluent Patois speakers included a number
of young women. Patois is by no means an exclusively male
domain.

Notes

1. This chapter is based on the findings of 'Patterns of Language in A
   British Black Community', funded by the Economic and Social
   Research Council, 1982–5.
2. All Black country nonstandard variants. *Ay* corresponds to standard
   English *isn't, day* to *didn't* and *bay* to *be*.

Chapter 5

Differences of sex and sects: linguistic variation and social networks in a Welsh mining village

Beth Thomas

Pont-rhyd-y-fen is a small industrial community, roughly equi-distant from the urban centres of Neath and Port Talbot in South Wales (see Fig. 5.1). Until the Second World War, this village survived as a Welsh language enclave in an area increasingly characterised by language shift to English. The homogeneous, close-knit society that existed in Pont-rhyd-y-fen while it was still a traditional mining community helped to maintain the use of the minority language. But, since the war, changes in employment, population and education – almost every aspect of community life – have led to the weakening of ties within the community and a widespread shift to English.[1] Today, only a third of the village's population is Welsh-speaking, compared with over 75 per cent in 1951. The majority of these Welsh speakers are in the 50+ age group, and belong to dense, multiplex social networks forged in the pre-war mining community. Generations raised since the war, in a period of social change and broadening of outlook, are predominantly English-speaking.

The importance of the close-knit social network as a mechanism of language maintenance has been demonstrated in a number of sociolinguistic studies.[2] In the case of Pont-rhyd-y-fen, network differences can account not only for the varying use of Welsh within the community, but also for variation within the community's spoken Welsh. The main focus of this paper will be the realisation of one particular phonological variable which is a feature of the dialect of east Glamorgan. In this part of South Wales, the long open vowel in monosyllables and stressed final syllables has two realisations: it is either a fully open [a:] or a fronted and raised [ɛ:]. Other South Wales dialects have only the [a:] form. So, for example, the Welsh word for *father* is

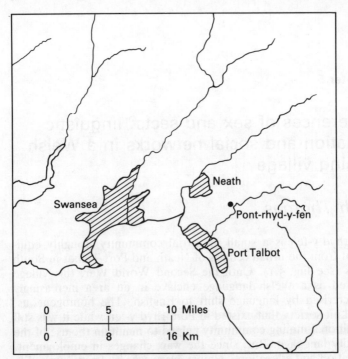

FIG. 5.1   Map of West Glamorgan showing the location of
            Pont-rhyd-y-fen

pronounced [ta:d] in most of South Wales, but [tɛ:d] in east
Glamorgan; the word for the Welsh language is [kəm′ra:g] in
South Wales generally, but [kəm′rɛ:g] in east Glamorgan, and
so on. The [ɛ:] variant is, however, fast disappearing, in part
because of a reduction in the numbers of indigenous Welsh
speakers in east Glamorgan, and in part because of its status as
a stigmatised feature of a low prestige dialect.

Geographically, Pont-rhyd-y-fen is in a marginal position so far
as this variable is concerned. The [ɛ:] variant is not heard in areas
to the west of the village, nor even in the next village down the
valley, whose inhabitants, incidentally, make fun of this feature
in the speech of people from Pont-rhyd-y-fen, comparing them
with sheep because 'they go meh meh all over the place'. Yet,
although this variant is a stereotype of Pont-rhyd-y-fen speech,
its use in the village is by no means general, but confined to a
minority of the community's Welsh speakers.

The total Welsh-speaking population of the village is about 250 people, of whom 54 were interviewed in a sociolinguistic survey of the community's spoken Welsh.[3] Although an attempt was made to elicit both interview and spontaneous speech styles from each informant in the sample, it did not prove possible in some cases to overcome the constraints of the interview situation and obtain examples of spontaneous speech. Most of the informants who had received further education fell into this group. However, 38 informants were more obliging, and it is their scores which form the basis of Table 5.1.

TABLE 5.1   Distribution of [ɛ:] variant by age, sex and style (median scores)

	Interview style	Spontaneous style
Men under 50	0	0
Women under 50	0	0
Men 50+	0	0
Women 50+	13	68

Scores for each individual were calculated in terms of the presence or absence of the [ɛ:] variant, as percentages. It can be seen from the table that the vernacular variant is found only in the speech of older women. Men of the same generation, and younger Welsh speakers of both sexes, make no use of it at all. Furthermore, in the 50+ age group, sharp differentiation between the sexes exists even within the same family, between brother and sister, and husband and wife, though the individuals involved are often unaware of this. In this community, it is the women who are the most conservative linguistically, not the men. This can, however, be explained in terms of differences in the nature of their social networks, and Pont-rhyd-y-fen's marginal location in relation to the geographical distribution of this phonological feature.

The social networks of both men and women of the older generation in Pont-rhyd-y-fen are very community-based. In their formative years, this was a highly self-sufficient working-class community. Its population was much higher than it is now, enabling the villagers to sustain numerous local social activities. There was much intermarriage within the community, this being reflected in the density of kinship ties between villagers. Of the 54 informants randomly selected, all but four of them were related to at least one other in the sample – some were related to as many as five or six. The majority of those aged 50 and over were also educated locally, remaining in the village school until they reached fourteen. For the men, employment was then available in local collieries, where they worked alongside neighbours and kinsmen, and men from two neighbouring communities. For the women, employment opportunities were very limited. Most girls on leaving school helped at home, or worked as seamstresses or domestic servants within the community.

However, although the social networks of both men and women of the 50+ age group are dense, multiplex and localised, those of the women are even more community-based than those of the men. The lives of the women revolve mainly around the home, the immediate neighbourhood and the chapel. All the female informants in the 50+ age group have spent the best part of their lives working within the community. A large proportion of them have never worked outside the home, and have even lived in the same house all of their lives. The social contacts and work experience of men of the same generation have been much more varied, especially since the colliery closures of the 1930s and 50s, and the diversification of industry since the war. Even when work was available locally, they worked with men from neighbouring villages, where the [ɛ] variant was not used.

As far as younger Welsh speakers are concerned, the social networks of both sexes are considerably less dense and multiplex than those of their elders. The village's population has decreased considerably since the 1930s, and is heavily biassed towards the older generation. Young people have difficulty in finding others of the same age and interests as them locally, and tend to socialise outside the community. The development of lighter industries has led to the greater employment of women outside the home. Educational changes have also affected social networks. Since 1950, all Pont-rhyd-y-fen children have left the village school at 11 years of age to finish their education elsewhere. And the establishment of a Welsh-medium primary school in the village further broadened social horizons by bringing in children from a wider catchment area. The social networks of this generation consist mainly of English speakers, with the few Welsh-speaking members coming from areas where the [ɛ:] variant is not a feature of the dialect.

Use of the [ɛ:] variant is therefore confined to the social group with the strongest neighbourhood ties, namely the older women. However, the group scores shown in Table 5.1 conceal the amount of variation within this group. There are women who are consistently high scorers in both styles, women who have consistently low scores in both styles, and others who show a great degree of style-shifting. The number of women of this age group in the original sample was not sufficient to discover any pattern to this variation. The data did, however, suggest that the geographical aspect might be important, as the vernacular variant seemed to be stronger at the eastern end of the village. More women of this age group were therefore interviewed to improve the geographical coverage.

The results can be seen in Figure 5.2, which gives the scores in spontaneous styles of 18 women, according to the area of their upbringing. The scores are arranged in a stem-and-leaf display, an exploratory technique devised by Tukey.[4] In this display, the centre column or 'stem' represents the tens, from 0 to 10 (i.e. from 0 to 100), while the units of each score are arranged opposite the appropriate 'ten' to give the 'leaves' to the right of the stem. The left-hand series of leaves shows where each informant was raised in the village.

Although the village of Pont-rhyd-y-fen is only about a mile long (see Fig. 5.3), the distribution of the [ɛ:] variant does show some geographical patterning in that all those raised at the western end of the village favour the [a:] variant, while almost all those raised at the eastern end favour [ɛ:]. But those women

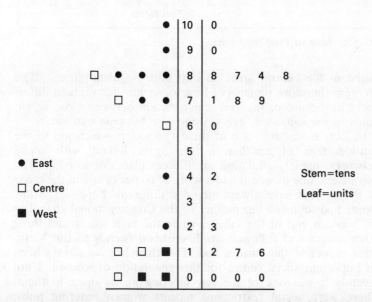

FIG. 5.2 Women 50+, spontaneous style, by area of upbringing

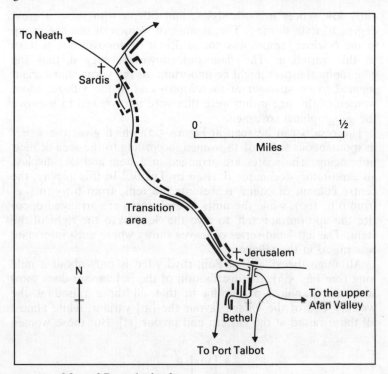

FIG. 5.3   Map of Pont-rhyd-y-fen

raised in the central area fall into both linguistic groups. The
problem therefore remains of how to account for marked differences in the use of the vernacular variant between close neighbours of the same sex, even in one case between two sisters.

In fact, it was the case of these two sisters which led to the
consideration of another factor, again linked with social
networks, namely affiliation to different places of worship. The
two sisters, one of whom had a score of 60 per cent and the other
of 17 per cent have always attended different chapels. The low
scorer had followed her mother to the Congregational chapel at
the western end of the village, while the high scorer and three
other sisters had followed neighbourhood friends to the Meth-
odist chapel at the eastern end. The chapels have always been
an important social centre for this generation of women. Until
recently it was one of the few meeting places open to them.
There were social restrictions against women entering pubs,
billiard rooms, and other social centres open to men. Girls from

very strict nonconformist backgrounds were forbidden to attend dances, or even to listen to dance music on the radio. Because of such restrictions, their networks of friends tend to be drawn either from their immediate neighbourhood or from a particular chapel.

There are three chapels in Pont-rhyd-y-fen (see Fig. 5.3) Sardis, the Congregational chapel at the far western end of the village, and Jerusalem and Bethel, for the Methodists and Baptists respectively, at the far eastern end. Membership of these chapels is territorially based. Chapel records show that they have always drawn most of their membership from their immediate neighbourhood, with Sardis servicing the western end, and Jerusalem and Bethel the eastern part of the village. In the centre, the catchment areas of the three chapels overlap.

Fig. 5.4 is based on the same data as Figure 5.2 but shows how the scores are distributed according to the informants' place of worship. It can be seen that all the high scorers attend the chapels at the eastern end, while those who worship at the western end are low scorers. There are three outliers, the most obvious being the woman from Bethel who is to be found in the same linguistic group as those from Sardis. She is in fact an outsider as far as the women of Bethel are concerned. She is the

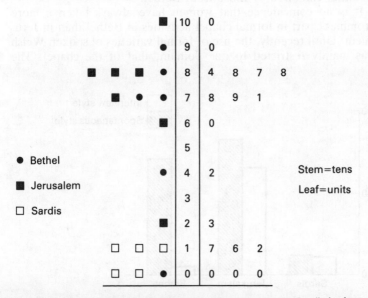

FIG. 5.4 Women 50+, spontaneous style, by chapel of upbringing

only one among them to have been raised in the centre of the village; she is neither related to them, nor friendly with them. Her neighbourhood ties are therefore stronger than her chapel ties, and this is reflected in her speech. The other outlier from Bethel, who does not have quite as high a score as her friends, is the only one among them to have had grammar school education, staying on at school until she was 18. The woman from Jerusalem with a score of 23 per cent was married to a man raised further west in the Swansea area, whose [ɛ:]-less dialect she considered much better than her own, and which she tried to emulate. Her father's family were also from the Swansea area. Affiliation to different chapels does, however, explain the variation in the scores of those informants raised in the centre of the village, and accounts for the linguistic behaviour of the majority of the women in the sample.

In spontaneous styles, the women from the two eastern chapels, Jerusalem and Bethel, behave similarly. However, when style-shifting is considered, further subdivision is revealed. Figure 5.5 shows clearly that the greatest style-shifters are the group from Bethel. The Sardis women are consistently low scorers in both styles. Although some degree of style-shifting occurs in the speech of women from Jerusalem, it is not comparable with the variation exhibited by those from Bethel.

It is no coincidence that women have always taken a more prominent part in formal chapel activities in Bethel than in Jerusalem. Until recently, the use of formal varieties of spoken Welsh was mainly restricted to one domain, that of the chapel. The

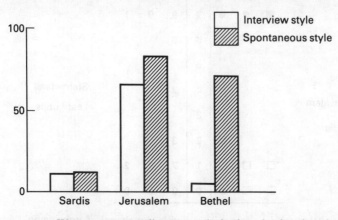

FIG. 5.5   Women 50+, median scores in both styles by chapel of upbringing

language of officialdom and education was English. Prestige varieties of Welsh have mainly been maintained by an elite of chapel officials, rather than by the highest in a hierarchy of social classes. The chapels were also local centres of Welsh cultural activities, such as *eisteddfodau*. Although most of the community took a passive part in the chapels' activities, active participants were in a minority. So it is interesting to note that two of the five style-shifters from Bethel are deaconesses and are therefore used to speaking Welsh in a public and formal context. One of them, by virtue of being a relative of a well known celebrity, has also recently been in great demand by the Welsh language media, taking part in both radio and television programmes. Three of the five women belong to the same family, noted in the community for its involvement in Welsh cultural activities. Only one of the style-shifters has no experience of public speaking. All of the style-shifters belong, however, to the same cohesive social group, based in the two streets adjoining the chapel.

It is also significant that some members of this group, through their involvement in Welsh cultural activities, have in recent years extended their social networks to include Welsh speakers from other areas, more importantly members of the Welsh establishment. This has meant exposure to more prestigious varieties of Welsh. Ironically, this has also meant exposure to the Welsh intelligentsia's current preoccupation with the preservation of local dialects. They are now faced with a situation where features they had previously thought of as 'slang' or a 'funny accent' have acquired a prestigious rarity value. When asked about the [ɛ:] variant in the interview, these women were the most eager to acknowledge the feature as part of 'our dialect', to admit to its use, and to express regret at the possibility that their dialect was dying out. One of the women even offered to prepare a monologue in Pont-rhyd-y-fen dialect so that I could record it. Paradoxically, despite her pride in the dialect, she did not use the most obvious marker of that dialect in the interview with me, nor in conversation with a friend from outside the area. With all the women from this group, the high [ɛ:] scores were recorded only in their interaction with family and friends from the neighbourhood.

To summarise, use of the [ɛ:] variant is confined to older women, whose social networks are more community-based than those of their male contemporaries and younger villagers of both sexes. The restriction of their work to the home did not necessarily mean participation in less cohesive social networks. They formed dense networks of friends and relations which were much relied upon for support and company, and which were largely centred on their membership of different chapels. Of the three chapels in Pont-rhyd-y-fen, use of the [ɛ:] variant is confined to those women who have networks based in the two chapels serving the eastern side of the village. For the sample from Jerusalem, use of Welsh is confined to interaction within the community, interaction with outsiders normally being in English. Although they did show some style-shifting, their scores for the vernacular variant were high in both interview and spontaneous styles. The greatest style-shifters were the women from Bethel. For them, like their contemporaries in Jerusalem, daily interaction is within the community. Unlike the Jerusalem women, however, they are also in sporadic contact with Welsh speakers from other areas and social backgrounds. It is these women who have greatest access to prestige varieties of Welsh and who are most able to shift in the direction of the interviewer. It can be argued that the linguistic behaviour of these women reflects the social groups with which they wish to be identified. They are no longer ashamed of this vernacular variant – for them it is a strong marker of local identity which they use freely among themselves and which they now regard almost as part of their local heritage. In the context of an interview, however, lack of the [ɛ:] variant in their speech perhaps indicates their identification with a wider network of culturally committed Welsh speakers to which they also belong.

The situation in Pont-rhyd-y-fen appears to go against the pattern found in other western industrialised communities, where women seem to lead the process of innovation (see, for instance, Trudgill 1972 and Milroy 1980). However, in a study of Mombasa Swahili, Russell (1982) noted a similar pattern to that found in Pont-rhyd-y-fen, with the women retaining the markers of 'insider' speech to a greater degree than the men. This supports the argument put forward by Cameron and Coates (Ch. 2) that vernacular culture is not exclusively a male phenomenon: the particular conditions obtaining in the Pont-rhyd-y-fen community have meant that a distinctive local vernacular variant is preserved, precisely, by older female speakers.

Notes

1. See Thomas (1987) for a full discussion of the process of language shift in this community.
2. See, for instance, Gal (1979) and Milroy (1980).
3. For a more detailed description of the fieldwork methods used, see Thomas (1982).
4. See Erickson and Nosanchuck (1979: 19–30).

PART TWO

Language and Sex in Connected Speech

Chapter 6

Introduction

Jennifer Coates

1. Quantitative and nonquantitative sociolinguistics

The essays in the second half of this book use approaches to the
study of language and society which lie outside the quantitative
paradigm. Some linguists have claimed that quantitative sociolinguistics *is* sociolinguistics (or 'sociolinguistics proper' as
Trudgill (1978: 11) calls it). In this book we take the wider view
that any research which improves our understanding of language
and society and the relationship between the two can be called
'sociolinguistic'.

We can loosely describe the chapters in this second section
with the term **the ethnography of communication:** this term refers
to work which looks at the way sociocultural knowledge is
revealed in the performance of speech events. Labov's well
known study of insults – 'Rules for ritual insults' (Labov 1972c)
– is a classic example of such work. As part of his work on Black
English vernacular, Labov analysed in detail the speech event
known as 'sounding' or 'signifying', as used by adolescent peer
groups in Harlem. He discussed both the *formal* characteristics
of ritual insults and also the *functions* that this speech event
served.

The ethnography of communication is ultimately concerned
with **communicative competence.** This concept originates in the
work of Dell Hymes (1971), who uses the term to refer to what
a speaker needs to know in order to be an effectively functioning
member of a speech community. Hymes argues that speakers
internalise far more than grammatical and phonological rules as
they learn to talk (these rules being what Chomsky means by
linguistic competence); speakers also internalise social and

cultural norms which enable them to use linguistic forms *appropriately*.

Communicative competence involves 'knowledge of when to speak or be silent: how to speak on each occasion: how to communicate (and interpret) meanings of respect, seriousness, humour, politeness or intimacy' (Milroy 1980: 85). Speakers also have to acquire an understanding of the social meaning of different linguistic varieties and different linguistic forms. For example, in a situation described by Gumperz (1982a), where a Black college student switched from standard American English to Black English in a college context, that switch had communicative significance: it was a comment to other Black students present that 'I'm just playing the game'. Another example is provided by Labov's Harlem study: as members of the (male) Black subculture, the adolescents studied by Labov are able to recognise the utterance *Your mother wears high-heeled sneakers to church* as a ritual insult, more particularly, as the opening move in a 'sound' (since opening moves normally refer to the addressee's mother).

The **speech event** is the basic unit of analysis in this framework. The following five chapters will cover speech events as varied as a radio phone-in, a TV discussion programme, classroom talk, wedding songs and informal conversation both in the workplace and the home. The focus on the speech event means that sociolinguistic work in this area is concerned with **connected speech**, and has strong links with both discourse analysis and conversational analysis. The emphasis on connected speech contrasts with quantitative sociolinguistics, where the main unit of analysis is the linguistic variable (usually a single phoneme, morpheme or lexical item).

2. Women and communicative competence

The ethnographic concern to chart the communicative norms of different communities was directed initially at working-class and ethnic minority communities. However, the notion that male and female speakers might in some senses constitute separate speech communities led to research in sex differences in communicative competence which paralleled sociolinguistic studies of sex differences in phonology, morphology and syntax.

Early work on 'women's language' or 'the female register' as it was variously called tended to be based more on casual observation and introspection rather than on empirical research. Moreover, the writers' perceptions of the topic were influenced by their preconceptions about male and female roles. None the less, these early works have been hugely inflential, and they certainly had the merit of making women's language an issue in linguistics. One of the aims of the second part of this book is to take a fresh look at such work: Chapters 7 and 8 are devoted to critiques of two of these early essays.

Since the publication of these early works, research focussing on women and language has become more sophisticated, with empirical research the norm. Studies have demonstrated significant differences in male and female usage of such features as interruptions, questions, polite forms, prosodic features, all of which are part of communicative competence. In the following chapters we present new evidence of sex differences in communicative competence in the following areas: tag questions (Ch. 7 and 8), interruptions (Ch. 8, 9, 10), minimal responses (Ch. 8, 10), linguistic hedging devices (Ch. 8), topic development (Ch. 8), verbosity (Ch. 9, 10).

The feminist project of 'redressing the balance' (see Cameron, Ch. 1) has meant that speech events associated with women are now seen as legitimate objects of study. (Until recently, all-woman discourse was completely ignored, by contrast with research on all-male speech events, such as ritual insults in Harlem, which were part of mainstream sociolinguistics.) In this second part, we present studies of two such all-female speech events – 'gossip' or all-female talk in a domestic setting, and Gujarati wedding songs, a speech event associated exclusively with women in the Gujarati-speaking community.

The fact that women and men differ in terms of their communicative behaviour is now established sociolinguistic fact. The problem remains of *explaining* such difference. How and why do women and men come to be in possession of different communicative norms? There are two conflicting views of women's status in society: one sees women as a minority group which is opressed and marginalised; the other sees women as simply different from men. The two main approaches to sex differences in communicative competence reflect these two views. The first – the **dominance** approach – interprets linguistic differences in women's and men's communicative competence as a reflection of men's dominance and women's subordination. The second – the **difference** approach – emphasises the idea that women and men belong to different subcultures: the differences in women's and men's communicative competence are interpreted as reflecting these different subcultures. Both approaches seem to yield valuable insights into the nature of sex differences, as the following chapters will demonstrate.

2.1 The dominance approach

Research adopting this approach sees the hierarchical nature of gender relations as the primary factor causing sex differences; women and men are described in terms of subordination and dominance. During the last 15 years, this approach has been used with different emphases. Early work, most significantly Robin Lakoff's 'Language and Woman's Place' (originally published in 1973), equated 'subordinate' with 'weak', and interpreted women's language as intrinsically inferior to men's (a deficit model). More recent work uses the notion of power to help illuminate gender inequalities while remaining more objective about the linguistic usage found to be typical of women or men.

Lakoff's essay was one of the earliest publications in the field. Her basic position is as follows: 'If the little girl learns her lesson well [learns 'special linguistic uses', i.e. female communicative competence], she is not rewarded with unquestioned acceptance on the part of society; rather, the acquisition of this special style of speech will later be an excuse others use to keep her in a demeaning position, to refuse to take her seriously as a human being' (Lakoff 1975: 5). This is a very strong version of the dominance approach. Unfortunately, Lakoff's essay relies on introspection and casual observation; it is not an empirical study. But her confident listing of particular linguistic forms as being markers of this demeaning 'special style of speech' has passed into folklinguistic lore and much subsequent research has referred to these forms as 'women's features' without question, and has assumed that they imply weakness.

Cameron, McAlinden and O'Leary's chapter (Ch. 7) is a reassessment of Lakoff's *Language and Woman's Place*. The authors point to two serious problems raised by Lakoff's argument. Firstly, they argue that the equating of a given linguistic form, such as a tag question or a 'weak' expletive, with one particular communicative function or meaning is questionable; they call this the **form and function** problem. Lakoff and many of her successors have taken such a one-to-one connection for granted; Cameron, McAlinden and O'Leary argue that, on the contrary, multifunctionality should be viewed as the unmarked case. Secondly they are critical of the explanatory framework adopted by Lakoff. They argue that Lakoff's elision of female gender with subordinate status is simplistic, and point to work adopting the alternative *difference* approach.

The second half of their chapter is devoted to two studies of the tag question using contrasting data bases. Their focus on the tag question is felicitous since it is this linguistic form, out of all those mentioned by Lakoff, which has come to hold the position of archetypal women's language feature. They show that the use of tag questions in conversation between equals seems to correlate with conversational *role* rather than with gender *per se*. Moreover, in the asymmetrical conversations they studied (where participants were not equal in status) certain sorts of tags were used more by *powerful* than by *powerless* participants, a finding which does not support Lakoff's claim that such forms are 'weak'. In conclusion, the authors argue that gender cannot be analysed in isolation from other non-linguistic variables, nor should it be concluded that linguistic features typical of subordinate groups are in themselves markers of subordination.

These theoretical concerns are taken up directly by Joan Swann in her chapter 'Talk control' (Ch. 9). As she says: 'Any interpretation of conversational features must actually be highly context-specific'. Moreover, she points to the difficulties of defining conversational features such as interruptions, and to the problem of interpreting differential usage of such features by women and men, once they are satisfactorily defined. To illustrate these problems, Swann presents an analysis of talk in the classroom, a context where it is of the utmost importance to expose the reproduction of inequalities. Children in the classroom are nominally equals, yet 'studies of classroom life have found many ways . . . in which girls and boys are treated differently'. Language is one of the means used to establish and perpetuate these inequalities. A crucial factor in patterns of classroom talk is the role of the teacher: for boys to dominate, teachers must in some way concur in this state of affairs.

To investigate how dominance is achieved in the classroom, Swann and her colleague made video-recordings of two 20-minute sequences of small group teaching in two primary schools. Their analysis of these video-recordings focusses on the mechanisms whereby turns are allocated and speaker change is negotiated, and on the roles played by different participants (girl pupils, boy pupils, teacher). Swann reports that, on average, boys contributed more to the sessions, both in terms of turns taken and number of words uttered, though in both schools there were examples of quieter boys and more talkative girls. In the first group, where spontaneous contributions were welcomed,

boys took advantage of this mode to chip in 41 times to the girls'
13. The boys' behaviour seems to have been directly related to
the teacher's *gaze* behaviour: analysis of the tape where the
teacher's gaze can be seen reveals that she looked towards the
boys for 61.3 per cent of the time. Moreover, the teacher looks
at the boys *at critical points*, when a question requires an answer.

In the second group, calling out was not encouraged, yet the
boys still dominated. The teacher selected the child whose hand
went up first. This favoured more confident pupils (often boys),
as did the teacher's gaze behaviour (she looked towards the boys
65 per cent of the time, and maintained her gaze towards them
when she began a question). Girl pupils, on the other hand,
themselves contributed to their own low level of participation by
raising their hands *after* the teacher had directed her gaze to the
pupil she intended to select.

Swann argues that these findings confirm that differences
between girls and boys are not categorical, since some boys are
quieter and some girls more talkative. However, the boys do
succeed in dominating classroom talk, though by different means
in the two classrooms surveyed. In other words, to be dominant,
a speaker has to use the resources available *in a given context*.
Swann also makes the point that boys' domination of classroom
talk is achieved in part at least through the behaviour of the girls
and of the teacher: in other words, she sees girls and teachers
as *colluding* in boys' dominance. Finally, Swann urges researchers
to make more use of video-recordings in the analysis of interaction, since nonverbal components of interaction such as gaze
direction or seating arrangements may turn out to have a vital
role in the achievement of male dominance.

Dominance in the *workplace* rather than the classroom is the
theme of Nicola Woods' chapter (Ch. 10). In this, Woods gives
an account of a project designed specifically to test whether it is
power or gender which is the critical variable in establishing
dominance. O'Barr and Atkins (1980) for example, have claimed
to prove that powerful participants (i.e. those with higher status)
are more forceful linguistically regardless of whether they are
male or female. Their research is, however, marred by their use
of Lakoff's 'women's language' features as an index of powerless
speech. Woods has chosen to confront the idea of dominance
head on by looking at those linguistic features which are used by
speakers to gain and hold the floor, and by showing in what ways
speakers' use of these forms correlates with their status and/or
gender.

The setting for her research is the workplace, where hierarchical rather than equal relationships are the norm. Her study focusses on six groups of three speakers: three groups consist of a male boss with one female and one male subordinate, and three of a female boss with one male and one female subordinate. The female bosses in the latter group are the same women as the female speakers holding second place in the hierarchy in the first set of triads. Woods's results show that it is gender rather than status that determines who holds the floor. Male speakers interrupted more, and were interrupted by others less, than female speakers; male speakers held significantly longer turns; male speakers received far more minimal responses (*mhm*, *yeah*, etc.). Overall, while occupational status did have some influence on floor-holding, it was men who dominated, whether they were boss or subordinate; being the boss did not lead to women holding the floor more than men.

A dominance model is clearly necessary for explicating Woods's findings. When a woman has higher status than a man, yet on linguistic measures fails to dominate her male subordinate, then we have to infer a gender hierarchy where male is construed as of higher value. (Woods's findings are not unique: West's (1984) study of doctors found that female, but not male, doctors were consistently interrupted by male patients.) However, the dominance approach is not always the most appropriate, as the studies described in the following section will demonstrate.

2.2 The difference approach
According to some researchers, women and men talk differently, or behave differently in spoken interaction, because they are socialised in different sociolinguistic subcultures. It is probably significant that this approach, the difference approach, emerged later than the dominance approach: it reflects a growing political awareness among linguists that by labelling men's language as 'strong' and women's language as 'weak', we were adopting an androcentric viewpoint. The difference, or subculture approach, attempts to investigate sex differences in communicative competence, and in particular women's language, from a *positive* standpoint.

Maltz and Borker (1982) draw up lists of 'women's features' and 'men's features', but unlike Lakoff they do not claim that these features reflect a power imbalance between the sexes, but that women and men have internalised different norms for conversational interaction. Using Gumperz's (1982b) work on inter-ethnic misunderstanding as a model, Maltz and Borker argue that the communicative competence of male and female speakers is acquired in single-sex peer groups. Communicative breakdown may occur in mixed interaction because women and men have different expectations of what taking part in a conversation entails, or because they interpret the use of specific features differently. Minimal responses, for example, are meant to signal 'I'm listening' in all-female groups, but 'I agree' in all-male groups. Women interpret men's rare use of minimal responses as lack of attention, while men are confused when women's minimal responses turn out *not* to signal agreement.

The difference approach has evolved as part of the explanatory framework for work on *same-sex* interaction. Where the quantitative sociolinguist has sampled the speech of randomly selected informants, ethnographers have always taken a more holistic approach, starting from the social group and its subculture. One of the earliest articles on all-female discourse was Deborah Jones's paper on 'Gossip: notes on women's oral culture' (1980). In this paper Jones offers a description of 'language use in women's natural groups': she looks at the settings in which women's interaction typically takes place, the kinds of topic discussed, the various kinds of talk which occur. Like Lakoff, Jones draws on personal observation rather than empirical data as evidence.

Chapter 8 in this second half presents a critique of Jones's paper, focussing in particular on the formal features of all-female discourse about which Jones claims little is known. Jones's account of gossip is tested against data consisting of recordings and transcripts of all-female conversations made by Coates. The author looks in detail at four formal features which seem to be typical of women's use of language in such discourse: topic development, minimal responses, simultaneous speech and epistemic modality (hedging devices). It is often claimed by those adopting a difference approach that the most significant difference between male and female communicative competence is that men's conversational style is based on **competitiveness**, whereas women's is based on **co-operativeness**. Coates argues that this claim is borne out as far as her women subjects are concerned: she shows that their characteristic use of gradual topic development, frequent and well placed minimal responses, overlapping speech, and linguistic forms which tone down what the speaker is saying all produce co-operative talk. When women talk, their chief aim is the maintenance of social relationships; this has priority over the exchange of information. Coates argues that women's goal of consolidating friendship is reflected in the way they talk: co-operative talk, the joint working out of a group point of view, takes precedence over individual assertions.

Is it possible to generalise from White, middle-class English women to women in general? How widespread is co-operativeness as a communicative norm among female speakers? Goodwin's (1980) work on Black girls and boys in Philadelphia; Abrahams's (1975) work on Black women in the US and Wodak's (1981) work on working-class adults in Vienna suggests that co-operativeness may not be restricted to one particular group of women, but this hypothesis remains to be tested.

Gossip belongs to the private sphere, as we would expect of a speech event associated with women. The division of public and private into male and female domains (see Hall 1985 and Coates Ch. 8) is reflected in the setting of male and female speech events. That is why the chapter by Viv Edwards and Savita Katbamna, 'The wedding songs of British Gujarati women' (Ch. 11), is of particular interest, since this highly valued public speech event is exclusively female. The data was collected by Katbamna, as an insider in the British Gujarati community, from Gujarati Hindu women in and around Harrow.

Edwards and Katbamna place their account of the wedding songs firmly in their social context, that is, in the context of Gujarati marriage rituals. These rituals have, inevitably, been modified in the British context, but the wedding songs remain and can be considered 'a living part of British Gujarati culture rather than a relic of village India'. The authors describe and analyse three different kinds of song: songs of solidarity, songs of insult and songs of conciliation, which mark the three main phases of the rite of passage which constitutes marriage. They argue that these songs provide insight into Gujarati social structure and values, and that there are healthy signs of adaptability to social change.

The tradition of wedding songs continues, according to the authors, because of the vital social function they fulfil in easing the transition of bride and groom from unmarried to married state, in bringing the family together, and in releasing the tension generated by the marriage. They hypothesise that these songs are the province of women because of women's role as mediators in the community, and because of the significance, both practical and emotional, of marriage to women. As Edwards and Katbamna put it: 'The turning upside down of the accepted norms of social behaviour before firmly reasserting the old order is particularly powerful when expressed by those members of society who traditionally exert least influence in formal settings.'

2.3 Do we need two approaches?

In sections 2.1 and 2.2 I have outlined and illustrated the two main approaches to male/female differences in communicative competence – the dominance approach, which stresses the hierarchical nature of gender relations, and the difference approach, which stresses subcultural differences between women and men. The sociolinguistic studies presented in the latter half of this book illustrate the need for both approaches. An analysis of classroom or workplace interaction which ignored the dimension of dominance and subordination would have little explanatory power. On the other hand, to insist that the conversational patterns typical of all-women groups can be explained by calling women an oppressed group is to do them less than justice. Moreover, the description of any speech event valued by the community which is the province of women clearly needs to be placed in a cultural context. While explanations involving a power dimension, and explanations involving subcultural factors are both needed, it would be simplistic to see them in an either/or relationship. Women's and men's subcultures are not divorced from prevailing power structures. As Cameron, McAlinden and O'Leary point out (Ch. 7), it is surely not coincidence that the conversational style associated with men is aggressive and competitive, while that associated with women is supportive and co-operative.

3. Conclusions

The second Part of this book, which looks at the question of language and sex from a more sociocultural perspective, addresses itself to various aspects of the subject. We present critiques of two of the more influential early studies of women's language, Robin Lakoff's *Language and Woman's Place* (see Ch. 7), and Deborah Jones's 'Gossip: notes on women's oral culture, (see Ch. 8). We also in this second Part present empirical data which we offer as a contribution to our knowledge of sex-differentiated communicative competence. These studies embrace a variety of speech events from formal public events such as Gujarati wedding songs to informal conversation in private. They cover interaction between equals (such as conversation between friends) and also asymmetrical interaction in settings as diverse as the classroom, the workplace, the TV studio. They also cover interaction in both mixed and single-sex groups.

In this second half, we also try to respond to Jones's claim that little is known about the linguistic forms typical of women's language. Our studies focus on a variety of linguistic forms: tag questions, minimal responses, interruptions and overlaps, verbosity, topic development, linguistic hedging devices. Finally, these studies contribute to the debate on explanations for sex differences in this area. Some of the work presented here adopts the *dominance* approach, some the *difference* approach. But none of the researchers whose work appears in the following chapters sees either of these approaches as wholly adequate: both power and subculture have to be incorporated into any reasoned account of male and female linguistic behaviour.

In order to sum up this introductory discussion, we can list the most important points which have emerged, and which need to be considered in future research.

1. Explanations of sex-differentiated language need to take a more sophisticated view of social behaviour and of social structure, acknowledging *both* dominance and subordination in gender relations *and* the different subcultures to which women and men belong and in which they internalise different interactional norms.

2. Research on the interactional norms typical of male and female speakers is still in its infancy, and relies on a very small body of data. We need a great deal more empirical work before we can say with confidence that a particular linguistic form is typical of women, or that a particular conversational strategy is typical of men.

3. Not only do we need more empirical evidence, we need to extend research to all sections of the community. Sociolinguists in this area have focussed too narrowly on White, middle-class women. We must turn our attention to girls and older women, to ethnic minority women, to working-class women, to women in different occupational groups.

4. The findings of research on same-sex and mixed interaction need to be kept carefully apart. The phrase 'women's language' can be used too glibly: we must not conflate the 'women's language' said to be typical of mixed interaction with the 'women's language' which characterises all-female discourse.

In the chapters which follow, these points will be debated. The various authors have their own perspectives on the subject of language and sex in connected discourse, but they all share the goal of putting women as speakers and the all-female speech events associated with them firmly on the sociolinguistic map.

Chapter 7

Lakoff in context: the social and linguistic functions of tag questions[1]

Deborah Cameron, Fiona McAlinden & Kathy O'Leary

1. Introduction

In recent years, there has been considerable interest in the differing linguistic behaviour of women and men. Work in this area has been of two main kinds: either it has concerned itself with phonological and grammatical variation, usually as part of a wider variationist project (e.g. Trudgill 1972; Cheshire 1982) or else it has involved the more 'holistic' exploration of gender-linked speech styles in natural or quasi-natural interaction. The use of politeness phenomena, questions and directives, patterns of floor-apportionment and hearer support are among the speech-style features that have been scrutinised for sex differences (e.g. Brown 1980; Goodwin 1980; Fishman 1980; Zimmerman and West 1975). Here it is this second 'speech style' strand we concentrate on. Drawing on empirical studies we have undertaken, we argue that it is time to reassess certain historical pre-occupations of researchers in this area; and we urge future investigators to be aware of the complexity of relations between linguistic form, communicative function, social context and social structure.

2. Work on women's style: the Lakoff hypothesis

Anyone surveying the literature on sex differences in speech style will immediately notice that the work of Robin Lakoff is frequently invoked as a reference point. Lakoff's well known study *Language and Woman's Place* (1975) is a general, wide-ranging discussion, by a linguist, of the English language as it is used by and about women. Originally published in a scholarly journal, the essay was reprinted in book form and has had considerable exposure and popular success, stimulating discussion both inside and outside linguistics.

From the point of view of today's researchers, the major drawback in Lakoff's work is its lack of any empirical basis. Rather than collecting corpora of male and female speech, Lakoff made claims based on her own intuitions and anecdotal observation of her peers' language use. Many of these claims have, not surprisingly, proved contentious. Yet, despite criticisms of Lakoff's methodology, the set of features she somewhat arbitrarily selected as markers of women's speech style continue to figure in research on sex differences. Because of the importance of *Language and Woman's Place* (*LWP*) at a time when the field had yet to establish itself, many later researchers apparently felt obliged to begin their own investigations with the so-called 'Lakoff hypothesis'. In some cases, especially in the mid-1970s, these researchers were specifically concerned to *test* the hypothesis. But even later on, as it became clear that matters were more complex than Lakoff had suggested, researchers did not always abandon the features to which *LWP* first drew attention. We shall see how this obsession with a particular set of features (and indeed with the question of whether Lakoff's substantive claims were right) has tended to leave important issues unresolved.

To start with, though, what exactly is the 'Lakoff hypothesis'? We can deal with it in two parts: substance and explanation. The substantive claims have to do with the existence of a typical female speech style. This style is marked, at least among educated North American English speakers, by the use of certain linguistic features such as hesitations, intensifiers and qualifiers, tag questions, rising intonation on declaratives, 'trivial' lexis and 'empty' adjectives.[2] What links these rather disparate linguistic phenomena is their alleged common function in communication: they weaken or mitigate the force of an utterance. For instance, Lakoff equates rising intonation on declaratives with showing tentativeness; tag questions are associated with a desire for confirmation or approval which signals a lack of self-confidence in the speaker. Qualifiers and intensifiers function in discourse as hedges. Thus Lakoff would assert that

(1a) *It's a nice day isn't it* (+ TAG)

is less assertive than just

(1b) *It's a nice day* (− TAG)

and analogously that

(2a) *I don't really want it* (+ QUALIFIER)

is less forceful than

(2b) *I don't want it* (− QUALIFIER).

According to Lakoff, a speaker who uses these mitigating features frequently will appear weak, unassertive and lacking in authority. From her claim that the features are typical of *women's* speech it follows that women appear weak and unassertive.

The association between femininity and unassertive speech is not in Lakoff's view coincidental. Her explanation of why women use a 'nonforceful' style links unassertiveness with social norms of womanhood. In a male-dominated society, women are brought up to think of assertion, authority and forcefulness as masculine qualities which they should avoid. They are taught instead to display the 'feminine' qualities of weakness, passivity and deference to men. It is entirely predictable, and given the pressures towards social conformity, rational, that women should demonstrate these qualities in their speech as well as in other aspects of their behaviour. Furthermore, the situation is self-perpetuating, since girls will tend to imitate the speech of their mothers and the female role models available in society.

Each of the parts of Lakoff's hypothesis seems to us to raise serious analytic issues quite apart from − and indeed prior to − the question of whether any evidence can be found for the substantive claims. Studies taking their cue from *LWP* have too often been preoccupied with its empirical dimension (do women use more of features x, y and z?) to the exclusion of crucial underlying problems. Two problems in particular merit detailed discussion.

3. Problems in the Lakoff hypothesis

3.1 The form and function problem

The first problem raised by *LWP* is the one we will refer to as the **form and function** problem, and it may be glossed as follows: how far is it possible to identify a recurrent form − say the tag question, or a rising nucleus − with some specific communicative function or meaning? Both Lakoff and her more empirically-minded successors have taken an identity of this kind pretty much for granted. In the case of tag questions, for instance, Lakoff makes it clear that unless a tag requests information unknown to the speaker, it is to be counted as signalling tentativeness and/or desire for approval. Stereotype counterexamples like

(3) *That was a silly thing to do, wasn't it* (parent to child)

spring readily to mind; but more seriously, it seems to us problematic to suggest that the communicative function of a syntactic form is either invariant or analytically transparent in all cases. Studies like our own, which deal with natural data, indicate the absolute necessity of considering forms in their linguistic and social context, not in general, and suggest that we should regard multifunctionality as the unmarked case – that is, in real talk most utterances do many things at once.

If accepted, though, this observation complicate research on sex differences in speech style, since unless we can map linguistic forms onto functions in the way Lakoff does, any claim that women use form x more than men begs the question 'so what?'.

Early attempts to investigate the Lakoff hypothesis empirically (Dubois & Crouch 1975; Crosby & Nyquist 1977) suffer to some degree from their failure fully to confront the form and function problem. Dubois and Crouch, for instance, sought to disprove Lakoff's claim that women use tag questions more often than men. Using data recorded at an academic conference, these researchers found men used tags far more than women. Yet on its own, this finding is surely unilluminating, since although it refutes Lakoff's general claim, it does not reveal why and to what extent she was wrong. Nor indeed does it explain Dubois and Crouch's own findings; for the explanation must depend on an account of what tag questions mean in different contexts. Do academic conferences make men more tentative than usual? Do tags serve some other purpose in a conference setting? Dubois and Crouch quite rightly conclude that in their data, tags do not indicate avoidance of commitment (a function which Lakoff had ascribed to some types of tag). But to deal intelligently with all the alternative possibilities, and with the range of meaning tags have across contexts, requires much greater awareness of the complexity of form-function relations, and the way these interact with context of situation. In the central part of this paper we will return to the form and function problem as it relates to tag questions in different contexts.

3.2 The problem of explanation

First, though, we need to examine another problem, this time in Lakoff's explanatory framework. As we have noted, Lakoff relates unassertive female speech to the norms of femininity which follow in turn from women's subordinate social position. While this is a plausible enough account, it is not the only possible one; it raises, in particular, the theoretical issue of whether gender role ('femininity') and status (defined in terms of a cluster of features like age, social class, sex, position in occupational and other hierarchies) should be conflated – and if not, whether one is more important than the other in determining or influencing an individual's speech style. Put crudely, is 'women's language' a consequence of being female, or of being subordinate, or some mixture of the two?

This is not an issue to which Lakoff is able to devote much discussion: it is clear that for her the most important aspect of 'women's language' is its association with weakness and subordination, but on the other hand she calls it *women's* language, that is, typical of women rather than other socially subordinated groups. Later writers, however, have reconsidered this: one well-known study (O'Barr & Atkins 1980) explicitly poses the question in its title, '"Women's language" or "powerless language"?'.

O'Barr and Atkins studied the speech of male and female witnesses in a Carolina courtroom. They were looking for features of Lakoff's 'women's language': exaggerated polite forms, hedges, intensifiers and tag questions (though in fact they had to discard this last variable since it turned out that witnesses seldom used interrogative forms). Briefly, when they quantified the use of 'women's language' features, O'Barr and Atkins found them not to be typical of all women, nor to be confined to the speech of women only. A better determinant of whether some individual scored highly on the features was his or her status, both in general (social class and occupation) and in relation to local courtroom norms (that is, experienced witnesses gained status from their knowledge of the expected procedure, and this showed up in their mode of speech). Several professional women who appeared as expert witnesses had lower scores than a number of men (i.e. used fewer 'women's language' features), while unemployed and blue-collar male speakers scored higher than a number of women. The high-scoring women tended to be unwaged 'housewives' or to be employed in low-status jobs.

O'Barr and Atkins concluded that 'women's language' is something of a misnomer: what they and Lakoff had been dealing with was a status-linked variety or 'powerless language'. The positive, though not overwhelming correlation they found between this variety and women speakers should arguably be explained as a consequence of the fact that women on average occupy lower status positions than men; nevertheless, the important factor is status rather than sex *per se*.

At the other end of the explanatory spectrum from O'Barr and Atkins, and implicitly from Lakoff, are those writers who argue that male and female speech styles are not primarily determined by power and status, preferring to see sex differences as deriving from the gender-specific subcultures that are formed in childhood play.

One article often cited in support of this position is Goodwin's (1980) study of children's directives in two Philadelphia peer groups. Goodwin's study relates directive usage to the differing organisation of male and female single-sex groups. Male peer groups are organised as hierarchical structures, and the resulting asymmetries in individual status are reflected in which boys use directives, and how: leading group members issue direct imperatives like *Gimme the pliers*, whereas subordinate members avoid such forms completely. Girls' peer groups are organised along different lines; there is less asymmetry and fewer direct commands are used. Instead the girls favour *suggesting* moves, commonly realised by the linguistic element *let's*.

Goodwin's findings fit in well with the folklinguistic belief that men have an aggressive and competitive speech style whereas women tend more to co-operative speech. The two sets of tendencies are sometimes said to be particularly marked in the 'natural' setting of single-sex talk (natural in the sense that for most children it is single-sex talk and play which are formative – the single-sex mode is the earliest they learn). Although on the face of it this point of view resembles Lakoff's since it also relies heavily on a notion of quite rigid and divergent gender roles which the sexes act out, there is a crucial difference in evaluation between followers of Lakoff and the 'subculture' theorists. For Lakoff, women's style is *deficient*, lacking authority and assertiveness. For subculture theorists like Jones (1980) it is *different*, but not deficient, and may indeed possess virtues of its own. The desire of some analysts to revalue what is thought distinctively female in speech style leads to an explanation of women's language not as the deplorable result of male dominance, but as a positive manifestation of female culture and values.[3]

The subcultural approach has been applied to miscommunications and interactional conflicts between women and men. Instead of regarding these as local instances of a more general power struggle, theorists like Maltz and Borker (1982) regard them as comparable to the misunderstandings which arise between speakers from different ethnic groups, who are often unaware that they are orienting to very different discourse norms. Drawing on the work of Gumperz (1982b), Maltz and Borker argue that women and men also have different discourse norms, since they typically acquire communicative competence in single-sex peer groups. An example they give is the interpretation of minimal responses, which women use more frequently than men (Hirschman 1974; Fishman 1980). For women, they say, these responses mean 'I hear you', whereas for men they mean 'I agree with you'. Thus women and men have different expectations about the incidence of minimal responses in talk. They tend to misinterpret each other, and this leads to frustration and communicative breakdown.[4]

The 'culture' versus 'power' argument is a significant one for researchers in the area of sex differences in speech style. We would argue, however, that it has often been posed in an over-simple way. On one hand, it is surely implausible to claim that the gender-specific subcultures posited by some analysts are quite independent of power structures. Can it be coincidence that men are aggressive and hierarchically-organised conversationalists, whereas women are expected to provide conversational support? On the other hand, the content of any group's speech style is unlikely to be reducible to their position in the social order. We will need to consider this whole debate further in the empirical case studies to which we now turn.

4. Empirical case studies

4.1 The tag question

The linguistic feature chosen here as a case study is one which has really got into the bones of the debate on language and sex since it was originally discussed by Lakoff, and we have had occasion to allude to it several times already in our theoretical discussion (above): the tag question. The idea that women use more tag questions than men because tags in many contexts indicate tentativeness and approval-seeking has passed out of the domain of academic speculation and into folklinguistic common sense, not excluding the folklinguistic common sense of feminists. How useful and accurate this view of tag questions is will now be considered using two separate studies of contrasting data bases.

4.2 Tag questions in casual conversation

4.2.1 Aims of the study

The first study is based on a corpus of nine texts of 5,000 words each from the Survey of English Usage (SEU) conversational corpus based at University College, London. Three texts involved male speakers only, three female speakers only, and three speakers of both sexes. Some 25 speakers were sampled altogether, the constraints of the SEU (which set out to collect examples of 'educated' British English usage, i.e. middle-class, mostly southern and overwhelmingly white English speech) ensuring a relatively homogeneous group in terms of social status. The aim of the study was to discover what sex differences, if any, existed in this group's use of tag questions.

Tag questions were defined formally as grammatical structures in which a declarative is followed by an attached interrogative clause or 'tag' where the first element of the declarative's AUX component (or dummy DO), usually with its original polarity reversed, and a pronoun coreferential with the original subject NP are 'copied out' – as in, for instance:

(4) *You were missing last week* / *weren't you* (SEU)

or, with polarity constant rather than reversed:

(5) *Thorpe's away* / *is he* (SEU).

Examples of tag questions from the 45000 words sampled were further coded for variation on a number of formal features: position (utterance-initial vs. utterance-medial), polarity (constant vs. reversed) and intonation (rising ($\nearrow$) vs. falling ($\searrow$) tone).

In addition to this formal analysis we attempted a functional classification of the tag questions in our data. Given our criticisms of mindless quantification, we were anxious to avoid merely comparing women's total usage of tags with men's without first ascertaining that they were using the structure in comparable ways; we were also interested in challenging Lakoff's very cut and dried, restrictive view of tag questions' functions: that unless they request information unknown to the speaker they should be treated as 'illegitimate', markers of tentativeness, a sign that the speaker has 'no views of his [sic] own' (Lakoff 1975: 17). This view has recently also been challenged by the New Zealand linguist Janet Holmes.

4.2.2 Analysing tag questions: the work of Holmes

Holmes (1984) is very much aware of what we have labelled the 'form and function' problem. She notes (1984: 52) that in discussions of sex differences in speech style:

> Most investigators have simply counted linguistic forms and compared the totals for women vs. men with very little discussion of the functions of the forms in the context of the discourse in which they occur.

In elucidating these functions, Holmes suggests (1984: 50):

> at least two interrelated contextual factors need to be taken into
> account, namely the function of the speech act in the developing
> discourse, and the relationship between the participants in the
> context of utterance.

Holmes's own analysis distinguishes two main functions of tag
questions which she calls **modal** and **affective**. Modal tags are
those which request information or confirmation of information
of which the speaker is uncertain; in Holmes's terms they are
'speaker-oriented', i.e. designed to meet the speaker's need for
information. Examples of this type from the Survey data include:

(4) *You were missing last week / weren't you* (SEU)

(6) *But you've been in Reading longer than that / haven't you*
(SEU).

'Affective tags' by contrast are addressee-oriented: that is, they
are used not to signal uncertainty on the part of the speaker, but
to indicate concern for the addressee. This concern can take two
distinct forms. On one hand, it can exemplify what Brown and
Levinson (1978) call 'negative politeness': a speaker may use a
tag to 'soften' or mitigate a face-threatening act. Holmes gives
the example:

(7) *Open the door for me, could you*

where the baldness of the directive is mitigated by the tag, and
the face-threat to the addressee correspondingly reduced. Tags
used in this way are referred to by Holmes as 'softeners'. On the
other hand, concern can be directed to the addressee's positive
face: rather than merely reducing possible offence, a tag may be
used to indicate a positive interest in or solidarity with the
addressee, and especially to offer her or him a way into the
discourse, signalling, in effect, 'OK, your turn now'. Holmes
labels this kind of tag 'facilitative'. Examples from the Survey
data include:

(8) *His portraits are quite static by comparison* \ *aren't they*
(SEU)

(9) *Quite a nice room to sit in actually* \ *isn't it* (SEU).

It is precisely this kind of 'facilitative' tag which Lakoff would
read as 'illegitimate', a covert request for approval. The speakers
of (8) and (9) express personal opinions and value-judgements
which in no way require confirmation from anyone else. Indeed,
for an addressee to disagree or withhold agreement here would

be markedly and noticeably unco-operative. Thus Lakoff would hold that the tag is uncalled-for and overly deferential. But Holmes finds this reading unsubtle and unhelpful. Facilitative tags may have no informational function, but they do have an important *interactional* function, that of drawing other participants into an exchange. To call this 'illegitimate' begs the question.

Holmes's analysis of the functions of tag questions allows her to modify the Lakoff hypothesis. As we know from studies like Dubois and Crouch's, it is not invariably true that women use more tags overall than men. But it might be plausible to suggest that they use more tags with affective meaning, especially facilitative tags. Women, after all, are allegedly 'co-operative' conversationalists who express frequent concern for other participants in talk; in mixed interaction it has been suggested that women are expected to do what Pamela Fishman has called 'interactional shitwork', – essentially a talk-facilitation task.

Holmes's own data support this modified hypothesis. She found that in her sample, 59 per cent of women's tags were facilitative compared to 35 per cent which were modal; for men these proportions were more or less reversed, at 25 per cent facilitative tags and 61 per cent modals (the remaining percentage for both sexes is accounted for by softeners, of which men in fact use a higher proportion. For actual values see Table 7.1, section 4.2.4 below).

In our own study we set out to investigate two questions: first, whether the modal/affective distinction could fruitfully be applied to data from the SEU; and second, whether the application of the distinction would yield findings on sex difference similar to those reported by Holmes.

4.2.3 Applying Holmes's framework to the Survey data

Although we did eventually classify all tag questions in our sample as either modal or affective, the task was not wholly unproblematic, and this in turn drew attention to difficulties in Holmes's own analysis. It is of interest to consider the problems we encountered, since they show the extent to which all analyses of this kind must inevitably be dogged by the form and function problem.

First of all, it was not always possible to assign specific examples to one or other of the modal and affective categories unambiguously. More precisely, there were instances where it seemed most satisfactory to analyse a tag as having some orientation to both speaker *and* addressee. Take, for example, (4) above:

You were missing last week ╱ weren't you

We eventually classified this as a modal tag, on the grounds that it called for confirmation of a fact the speaker was not sure of. But arguably it also has an element of the softener about it, since either the bald declarative

You were missing last week

or the direct polar interrogative

Were you missing last week

would tend to sound like accusations, and thus to threaten the addressee's face. The tag could be perceived as mitigating this face-threat.

It seems to us that examples like (4) underline the essential multifunctionality of utterances in discourse. Linguists have often underestimated the interpersonal, as opposed to referential functions of language (a point also made in a similar connection by Coates 1987); given the importance of 'facework' in interaction, we may doubt whether there is such a thing as a purely modal or speaker-oriented tag question. Holmes's framework, however, compelled us to make a somewhat artificial choice between stressing the modal and the affective aspects of (4) and other similar examples.

Faced with this sort of choice, we were often influenced by the formal feature of rising vs. falling tone (i.e. rising tone, all other things being equal, was taken to signal a genuine, that is modal, question). But this criterion, it should be noted, is hardly infallible. Our sample contained a significant number of counter-examples such as:

(10) *One wouldn't have the nerve to take that one ╱ would one* (SEU)

where the speaker uses rising tone although he is making a value-judgement like those in (8) and (9), rather than querying a matter of fact (the topic of (10), incidentally, is a nude picture). Conversely

(11) *The provost is addressing us tomorrow ╲ isn't he*

seems in context to be a request for confirmation in spite of the falling tone. Overall in our data, 25 per cent of women's tags are modal and 40 per cent of men's; but only 11 per cent of women's tags and 18 per cent of men's have rising tone. So it is clear that the status of a tag as modal cannot simply be read off from its intonation.

To sum up, then, we did find some difficulty in applying Holmes's framework to our data (and we will argue later that the difficulties are compounded if one examines data from contexts other than casual conversation). Tag questions, like other linguistic forms, are characterised by complex multifunctionality and diversity of meaning, so that a certain degree of arbitrariness is to be expected in any functional classification.

4.2.4 Sex-difference findings

The 45,000 words sampled from the SEU gave us a database of 96 tag questions, of which 36 were produced by women and 60 by men. When these 96 tags were analysed as either modal or affective, subject, of course, to the reservations outlined above, the expected sex difference did appear. (See Table 7.1.)

TABLE 7.1   Tag questions in casual conversation

	Holmes 1984		SEU	
	F	M	F	M
Modal	18 (35%)	24 (61%)	9 (25%)	24 (40%)
Affective				
Facilitative	30 (59%)	10 (25%)	27 (75%)	36 (60%)
Softeners	3 (6%)	5 (13%)	—	—
Total tags	51	39	36	60

It is noticeable that while our findings for women are more decisive than Holmes's – that is, the women in the SEU sample lean even more firmly towards facilitative rather than modal tags – our findings for men's speech are less decisive. Men in the SEU sample used far more facilitative tags than those whose speech was sampled by Holmes. On examination, we discovered an interesting factor which may have skewed the scores for the SEU men: three speakers in our sample texts had been aware that recording was taking place, and these speakers – two of whom were men – had abnormally high scores for facilitative tags. It may be that their speech reflected a concern to elicit as much talk as possible from other participants, in order to generate as much data as possible for the Survey. In other words, these speakers had either consciously or unconsciously taken on the role of conversational 'facilitator'. If their contribution were discounted altogether, the incidence of facilitative tags among men would fall by around 6 per cent (though this is not enough to account for the considerable difference between our results and Holmes's).

What, if anything, do our findings suggest? One hypothesis which they seem to point towards (though obviously it would need to be more rigorously tested) is that the use of facilitative tags correlates with conversational role, rather than with gender *per se*. Where men take on a facilitating role they are able to produce large numbers of facilitative tags.

Both Holmes (1984) and Fishman (1980, 1983) have claimed that the role of facilitator in conversation is taken on (at least in casual conversation) more frequently and markedly by women than by men. The SEU findings do not necessarily lead us to dispute the validity of that claim. Nevertheless, future research must take very seriously the possibility of an intervening variable between gender and language use. This was one of the points we bore in mind in analysing the data from our second study of tag questions in context.

4.3 Tag questions in asymmetrical discourse

Our second study deliberately set out to introduce the variables of conversational role and differential status in addition to the variable of gender which we had considered in the first study. We had a reason for introducing these variables apart from the suspicions raised by the SEU findings: we wanted to pursue certain claims about tag questions put forward not by sex difference researchers but by discourse analysts investigating so-called 'unequal encounters'.

4.3.1 Unequal encounters and the functions of tag questions

If the tag question has been treated fairly unproblematically in sex-difference research as a marker of tentative or 'powerless' language, recent discourse studies are equally unambiguous in citing it as a marker of power and control in talk. Such contradictory positions on the same linguistic form will bear closer examination; we will begin by explaining the discourse analysts' perspective in more detail.

Discourse and conversation analysts of various theoretical inclinations agree that questioning is generally a powerful interactional move, because it obliges the interlocutor to produce an answer (in Conversational Analysis terms the 'second pair-part' of an 'adjacency pair') or to be accountable for its absence. Furthermore, if we consider Gricean principles, a question must constrain the addressee not only to respond, but to respond in a manner which is conversationally *relevant*: in other words, questions limit what the addressee can say.

Given these conditions, it is not surprising that students of 'unequal encounters' – that is, speech situations where one participant is institutionally invested with rights and obligations to control talk, as in courtrooms, classrooms, consulting rooms and boardrooms, for example – have found that the 'powerful' participants, people like magistrates and doctors, use extraordinarily large numbers of questioning moves in talk.[5] Furthermore, they have noted that 'powerless' participants *avoid* questions: they orient to the rule which says it is their business to produce replies. Where this rule is violated – when a defendant in court asks the magistrate a question, for instance – the response may be silence, interruption or an explicit rebuke to the effect that 'I'm asking the questions here' (Harris 1984).

As well as noting the general interactional power of questions, discourse analysts have pointed out that some types of interrogative by virtue of the grammaticalised and lexicalised expectations they encode, are more constraining than others. For instance, if a question contains a completed proposition, this takes more interactive work to challenge than it does to assent to; the consequence is that respondents tend to produce confirmations of the embedded proposition. Question forms which have this effect are known as 'conducive': and according to analysts like Hudson (1975) and Harris (1984), tags are preeminent among conducive question forms. We can see this easily by looking again at the invented example (1a):

>   *It's a nice day isn't it*

a remark which contains the complete proposition *it's a nice day*. It would indeed be odd to reply to this in the negative. The polar interrogative

>   *Is it a nice day*

in contrast is less conducive, permitting either a yes or no answer. This account of tag questions effectively reanalyses them as highly assertive strategies for coercing agreement, and not indications of tentativeness. It helps to explain why tags are so popular with the powerful participants in unequal encounters; Harris, for example, found them strongly favoured by magistrates, who would commonly make remarks along the lines of

(12) *You're not making much effort to pay off these arrears, are you?*

The analysis of examples like (12) incidentally marks another area of disagreement between us and Janet Holmes. Holmes analyses tags in utterances such as (12) as softeners: *are you* supposedly mitigates the extremely negative impact of the accusation *You're not making much effort*. But we would favour an alternative analysis in which the tag was perceived as a way of *increasing* the addressee's humiliation. Not only is the defendant addressed in (12) being accused of bad faith and idleness, he is also being invited (in an extremely conducive manner) to agree with the magistrate's assessment of his behaviour. This and similar examples (cf., for instance, (3) above) remind us of the stereotype military exchange '"You're an 'orrible little man, Smith, what are you?" "An 'orrible little man, sir!"'.

To summarise, then, the 'unequal encounters' strand of work on discourse presents us with an alternative hypothesis to the one usually entertained in relation to tag questions by sex difference researchers. This hypothesis is that tag questions function as an interactional resource of the *powerful* rather than the powerless in conversation. Looking more closely at this possibility might throw light on the problem of explanation (see section 3.2 above). Is women's use of facilitative tags a function of their powerlessness, their role in conversation, or of subcultural norms of female peer groups? (Of course, it is possible that unequal encounters differ markedly from ordinary talk in terms of what tag questions are used to accomplish; the form and function problem must therefore be borne in mind.)

4.3.2 The asymmetrical discourse study

Our second study used a data base of nine hours' recorded unscripted talk from three different broadcast settings: a medical radio phone-in where the participant roles were those of doctor and caller/client; classroom interaction recorded for Open University educational TV, in which the salient roles were those of teacher and pupil; and a general TV discussion programme, in which the roles were those of presenter and audience.

These settings were chosen because they conformed to the criterion for unequal encounters: in each case, one participant was clearly institutionally responsible for the conduct of the talk (and in two out of the three cases, this participant also had more power and status measured in terms of social class, occupation and age; the TV presenter was the exception, since studio audience members and invited guests varied widely in their social status, some of them being on a par with the presenter, others clearly subordinate to her). On the other hand, the settings involved quite varied interactional tasks which we hoped would give interesting insights into the functions of tag questions in different contexts. We sampled the broadcasts in such a way as to balance the numbers of women and men among both 'powerless' and 'powerful' speakers. As in the first study, we picked out all instances of tag questions from the data and analysed them using Holmes's framework of functions. We then broke the results down by the two variables of gender (male vs. female) and power (powerful vs. powerless). The results are shown in Table 7.2.

TABLE 7.2   Tag questions in unequal encounters

	Women		Men	
	P'ful	P'less	P'ful	P'less
Modal	3	9	10	16
	(5%)	(15%)	(18%)	(29%)
Affective				
Facilitative	43	0	25	0
	(70%)	—	(45%)	—
Softeners	6	0	4	0
	(10%)	—	(7%)	—
Total		61		55

What conclusions can be drawn from Table 7.2? First, we can see that it does support the findings of the previous study and those of Holmes in as much as men score higher on modal tags and women on affective ones, especially facilitatives. In this study it is women who use more tags overall, but at 61 to 55 the difference is not particularly striking.

What *is* striking is the difference between powerless and powerful participants' scores, especially in the affective category. No powerless person of either sex uses either facilitative or softening tags in any of the three settings. On the other hand, in the modal category it is powerless speakers who score higher by a proportion of two to one. If we stick to the preconception so prevalent in sex-difference research, that facilitative tags are used by powerless speakers whose subordinate position forces them into 'interactional shitwork', then this pattern is surely rather unexpected. How then can it be explained?

In our view, the results of this second study strongly support the claim of discourse analysts like Harris that tag questions are associated with the rights and responsibilities of 'powerful' speakers – but this is only true, it appears, of affective or addressee-oriented tags: the use of modal tags to confirm information does not appear to be a 'powerful' move, at least not in all instances. We can provide more detailed support for our conclusions by examining the uses to which different types of tag are put in the asymmetrical discourse sample.

Facilitative tags are most commonly used to get other participants to speak at some length. It is therefore not surprising to find they are favoured especially by the television presenter. Consider, for instance, the following example, in a discussion of why boxing continues to be popular:

(13) PRESENTER: *It's compulsive, isn't it* (elicits long reply from guest).

Softeners, as Holmes observes, mitigate criticism and therefore face-threat to the addressee, as is clear from the following examples:

(14) *You're going to cheat really, aren't you* (teacher to pupil)
(15) *That's a lot of weight to put on in a year, isn't it* (doctor to caller).

But what these examples also make clear is that powerful participants are much more likely to be in a position to criticise in the first place. Criticising is part of the role of teachers, and to some extent doctors; it is not supposed to be the business of pupils or clients, as can readily be appreciated if we try to imagine a pupil uttering (14) or a patient (15).

Modal tags are less clear-cut in their functions; but on close examination an interesting difference emerges between the modal tags used by powerful and powerless participants in our sample. The doctor in particular tended to use them to establish or summarise the facts of a case, cutting off the caller's narrative when this threatened to ramble:

(16) *It's become notorious has it* (doctor to caller, talking about caller's crush on a teacher, the 'problem' she has phoned about).

Powerless speakers by contrast tended to use modal tags in order to request reassurance, particularly in the classroom and medical contexts:

(17) *It is this one isn't it* (pupil to teacher)
(18) *I shouldn't have bothered my GP with it, should I* (caller to doctor).

The context of situation is obviously relevant here; the higher scores on modal tags obtained by powerless speakers must reflect the fact that our data were taken from two settings in which reassurance is commonly sought.

5. Conclusion

What have these two case studies of the tag-question form revealed? First of all, that the relation between linguistic form and communicative function is not a simple thing, and we cannot state *a priori* what tag questions do, even using something like Holmes's modal/affective distinction. This should make future researchers rather wary of the line of argument popularised by Lakoff, that if women use form x more than men we should seek an explanation of this in terms of the invariant communicative function of x.

Secondly, our findings suggest that the patterning of particular linguistic forms may be illuminated by a consideration of a number of variables, not just gender. These include the role taken by participants in interaction, the objectives of interaction, participants' relative status on a number of dimensions, and so on. It needs to be borne in mind generally that 'women' do not form a homogeneous social group. Gender is cross-cut with other social divisions and their relative importance is affected by the specifics of the situation (for instance, in a courtroom or class-room occupational role is likely to be more salient than any other social variable).[6]

Finally, a question which these studies have not resolved, but which in our opinion they certainly pose, is whether the role of conversational facilitator, which appears to favour the use of some types of tag in both casual conversation and unequal encounters, is a subcultural norm of all-female groups, a burden shouldered by subordinate speakers, or a strategy used to control ongoing talk – or, of course, whether it is all of these things at different times and in different settings. The possibility that women's more frequent use of facilitative tags could be a marker of control over conversation rather than one of responsibility for 'interactional shitwork' may appear to go against the grain of feminist studies. But this is surely something that merits a re-assessment. One of Lakoff's least helpful legacies is the tendency towards automatically identifying the linguistic strategies used by subordinate groups as *ipso facto* markers of subordinate status. No feminist would dispute that women are a subordinate group; but subordinate groups do after all negotiate and struggle against the conditions of their oppression. Certain aspects of their social behaviour might profitably be analysed not as a simple demonstration of those conditions, but as a complex way of coping with them, or even a mode of resistance to them. In order to move beyond the first phase of language and gender research represented by pioneers like Robin Lakoff, we must develop a more sophisticated view of the complexity of both linguistic and social behaviour.

Notes

1. This paper is based on two studies of tag questions by Fiona McAlinden (casual conversation study) and Kathy O'Leary (asymmetrical discourse study), respectively. We would like to acknowledge the assistance of Jennifer Coates in designing McAlinden's study. An earlier version of this paper was delivered to the Linguistic Circle of Oxford in May 1987, and we are grateful to all who made comments on it there.
2. Obviously, it would not be the case that these particular formal features marked 'women's language' in every speech community, or even in every Anglophone speech community (thus it has been pointed out, for instance, that rising intonation on declaratives is wholly unremarkable in many varieties of English, including Tyneside and Australian, and doubtless similar examples could be found for each of Lakoff's features).
3. Not all analysts who see women's language as related to male dominance would also regard that language as 'weak' or 'deplorable'. Pamela Fishman (1980) holds, for example, that women are skilful conversationalists partly because they are required to negotiate the unco-operative behaviour of dominant males.
4. Unfortunately, however, Maltz and Borker do not follow Gumperz (1982b) in testing out these differing perceptions empirically with samples of informants from male and female groups. Their argument concerning minimal responses cannot, therefore, be taken as proven.
5. 'Powerful' and 'powerless' are in scare quotes here to indicate that they should be taken as descriptions of the relation between participants in the particular setting under consideration, rather than general descriptions. For instance, when a brain surgeon appears before a magistrate charged with a motoring offence, she is 'powerless'; when the judge consults her about his recurrent headache in a medical context, their relative positions are reversed. Their (high) social status in general terms remains the same throughout, however. (On the other hand, it needs to be pointed out that the vast majority of people who appear in court, consult a doctor, etc. are not only 'powerless' in that setting in our terms, but also of a lower social status than the 'powerful' participant.)

6. Though research suggests this generalisation may not apply to every linguistic feature without exception. For instance, Nicola Woods (Ch. 10) finds that gender is a better predictor of who will dominate the floor than occupational status is, even in a work setting. In the case of interruption, verbosity, minimal response etc., the case for an intervening variable between language use and gender is less persuasive than for tag questions. We do not find this a worrying anomaly, though, since there is no theoretical reason to suppose that all gender-linked differences proceed from exactly the same causal factors.

Chapter 8

Gossip revisited: language in all-female groups

Jennifer Coates

1. Introduction

During the last ten years, interest in, and knowledge of, the relationship between language and sex has grown enormously. But attention has focussed on sex *differences*: sociolinguistic research has aimed to quantify differences in women's and men's usage of certain linguistic forms. The linguistic forms examined range from phonological or syntactic variables to interactive forms such as interruptions, directives and questions. Where the latter are concerned, a majority of researchers have drawn their data from mixed interaction (that is, interaction involving both male and female speakers); research has rarely focussed on women in single-sex groups. As a result, we know little about the characteristics of all-female discourse. Worse, we accept generalisations about 'the way women talk' which derive from women's behaviour in *mixed* groups, groups where the differential use of linguistic features such as interruptions, directives or questions is part of the social process which maintains gender divisions.

Deborah Jones's paper, 'Gossip: notes on women's oral culture' (1980), was a landmark. While Jones was not the first to focus on all-woman interaction (cf. Abrahams 1975; Kalcik 1975; Aries 1976; Jenkins & Kramer 1978), she was the first to locate her analysis firmly in the sociolinguistic field. Jones glosses 'female oral culture' as 'language use in women's natural groups' (using 'natural' to refer to groupings which in our *culture* are construed as 'natural'). Her paper offers a description of such language use in terms of the relations between setting, participants, topic, form and function, following Ervin-Tripp (1964). The strength of Jones's paper is that it puts women talking to women firmly centre-stage; its weakness stems from the lack of empirical data. Her common-sense description of the setting, participants and topics typical of all-woman talk provides a clear set of norms to be tested in further research. Her statement that 'Little is known about any distinctive formal features of women's language in all-female groups' is a challenge to linguists which this paper will take up.

Since the publication of Jones's paper, some linguists have developed the notion, originally used in inter-ethnic communication studies, that linguistic differences might be the result in part of subcultural differences rather than simply a reflection of dominant–subordinate relationships. Work adopting this model has explored miscommunication between the sexes (e.g. Maltz & Borker 1982; Tannen 1982, 1987). Such work makes the assumption, either implicitly or explicitly, that the conversational strategies which lead to miscommunication in mixed groups are acquired and developed in single-sex groups. But this assumption is unverified. The evidence presented in the few studies available (Kalcik 1975; Aries 1976; Goodwin 1980; Wodak 1981) is hardly conclusive (but does suggest that such conversational strategies may not be restricted to white middle-class women). We still know very little about the norms of spoken interaction in single-sex groups.

While they lack detail, the papers listed above all draw on a notion of **co-operativeness** to characterise all-female interaction. Early work on women's language had labelled it as 'tentative' or 'powerless'. More recently, and in reaction to this, there has been a move to value women's language more positively, using terms such as 'co-operative'. This is laudable; but in order to avoid the creation of new linguistic myths, it is important that such claims are substantiated by linguistic evidence.

In this Chapter, I want to analyse in detail part of a corpus of conversation between women friends. The corpus is small (135 minutes of running text), and the approach used is qualitative rather than quantitative.[1] I want firstly to see whether the evidence supports Jones's general claims, secondly to establish what formal features are typical of all-woman discourse, and thirdly to explore the notion of co-operativeness.

2. The data

I recorded a group of women friends over a period of nine months during 1983–4. These women were an established group who met once a fortnight at each other's houses in the evening to talk. I had belonged to this group since 1975, when it began to meet, and I recorded my friends surreptitiously each time it was my turn to have the group to my house during the period in question. All participants were informed subsequently that recordings had been made, and they agreed to this material being used for research purposes.[2] I shall discuss this data in relation to Jones's five headings, dealing briefly with setting, participants and topic, and at greater length with formal features and functions.

2.1 Setting

Jones follows Ervin-Tripp (1964) in using the term **setting** to cover both time and place. She identifies the private domain as the **place** for women's talk, and names the home, the hair-dresser's, the supermarket as typical locations. Her identification of the private sphere as the setting for women's subculture seems to me to deserve more emphasis than she gives it. The division between public and private as we now understand it was established at the beginning of the nineteenth century (see Hall (1985) for an account of the historical background). As the division became more highly demarcated, patterns of gender division also changed: 'men were firmly placed in the newly defined public world of business, commerce and politics; women were placed in the private world of home and family' (Hall 1985: 12). This split was to have significant sociolinguistic consequences.

Jones describes the setting of gossip in terms of **time** as brief and fragmented: 'Time to gossip is usually snatched from work time' (1980: 194). The claim that snatched episodes are an intrinsic feature of gossip seems debatable, and depends too heavily on seeing women as mothers with small children. Old women, for example, sit on park benches or in social clubs, chatting for extended periods; adolescent girls often congregate on neutral territory (not home or school) and have considerable spare time in which to talk, especially if they are playing truant from school (see Cheshire 1982). Even mothers with small children meet in settings where the quality of the talking cannot be defined as 'snatched' – outside the school gate at the end of the day; waiting in the clinic to weigh the baby; at the mother and toddler group. According to Milroy, in traditional working-class communities such as Belfast, 'speakers valued various kinds of conversational arts very highly. *Many hours were spent simply chatting*' (my italics) (Milroy 1980: 100). Of course, some interaction between women which we would want to label as typical women's talk is brief, but it seems that length of time is not a salient feature of gossip.

The setting for the conversations I recorded was the living room of my home in Birkenhead, Merseyside. People sat on sofas or on the floor around the gas fire, drinking wine. Sessions lasted three hours or more, starting at about 9.0 in the evening. Food was served about half way through the evening; this was usually bread and cheese, but sometimes something more elaborate such as home-made soup or pizza.

2.2 Participants

'Gossip is essentially talk between women in our common role *as* women' (Jones 1980: 195). Jones argues that gossip arises from women's perception of themselves as a group with a great deal of experience in common. The members of the women's group I recorded are white, middle class, aged in their late 30s and early 40s. The group was formed (in 1975) at a time when all members had children still at school, and some had babies (who attended in carry cots). The group's *raison d'être* shifted gradually over the years: it initially provided a support network for mothers with young children; it now encourages these same women in their struggle to establish a career in their middle age. Urwin (1985) has commented on the importance for young mothers of friendships with other women. The need for contact with other women at various stages of one's life, not just as young mothers, is certainly borne out by the Birkenhead group which has now existed for 12 years.

2.3 Topic

Jones claims that the topics discussed by women are crucially related to their roles as wives, girlfriends and mothers. This claim seems to me to be over-strong, and again to overemphasise the place of motherhood in women's lives. The conversations that I recorded cover a wide range of topics, from discussions of television programmes, to mothers' funerals and child abuse. However, as I have commented in an earlier paper (Coates 1987), it seems to be typical of all-women groups that they discuss people and feelings, while men are more likely to discuss things. This finding fits Jones's general claim that 'the wider theme of gossip is always personal experience' (1980: 195).

3. Functions

Unlike Jones, I shall discuss the functions of gossip before I discuss its formal features, since I want to argue that the linguistic forms which characterise women's interaction can be explained in terms of the functions they serve. Jones's section on functions is weak: she merely catalogues four different types of gossip. I want to use the term **function** in relation to the **goals** of all-woman interaction. All-woman conversation, like most informal interaction between equals, has as its chief goal the maintenance of good social relationships.

Grice's conversational maxims (Grice 1975) assume that refer-ential meaning is all-important, and that speakers' only aim is to exchange information. The falsity of this assumption has been demonstrated by Lakoff (1973) and discussed by many other linguists subsequently (e.g. G. Brown 1977; Leech 1983; Tannen 1984). The distinction between public and private spheres, discussed in section 2.1, leads to a distinction between public and private discourse. In public discourse, the exchange of infor-mation is an important goal. Male speakers in our culture are socialised into public discourse, while female speakers are social-ised into private discourse (cf. Gilligan 1982; P. Smith 1985; G. Wells 1979). Until recently, the androcentric view that infor-mation-focussed discourse should be the object of linguistic analysis was not challenged. In private discourse, the exchange of information is not the chief goal. I hope to show in the central section of this Chapter that the formal features which are typical of women's language in all-female groups can be explained by direct reference to the functions of such interaction, that is the establishment and maintenance of social relationships, the re-affirming and strengthening of friendship.

4. Formal features

I shall examine in detail four aspects of the interactional pattern found in the all-female conversation I recorded. I shall look at topic development, at minimal responses, at simultaneous speech, and finally at epistemic modality. I have chosen to concentrate on these aspects of women's talk because they have been picked out by other writers as markers of co-operative style.

4.1 Topic development

It has become a truism in accounts of women's discourse that women develop topics progressively in conversation (see Maltz & Borker 1982: 213). Yet, as far as I know, this claim has not been supported by empirical evidence. The claim is multifaceted: women are said to build on each others' contributions, preferring continuity to discontinuity, and topic shift is supposed to occur gradually (rather than abruptly, as in all-male conversation). Consequently, the discussion of a single topic can last for some time (up to half an hour according to Aries 1976: 13).

In order to examine the nature of topic development in all-female conversation, I shall analyse one episode in detail from one of my recordings. This passage is about mothers' funerals and lasts just under 4½ minutes. There are five participants. The structure of the funeral extract is as follows:

1. A introduces topic;
2. B tells anecdote on same theme;
3. C tells another anecdote on same theme, leading into:
4. general discussion;
5. D summarises;
6. A has last word.

In musical terms, (1), (2) and (3) form the exposition, (4) is the development, (5) the recapitulation, and (6) the coda. The development section is by far the longest (2 minutes 47 seconds). This pattern of topic development is typical of the material I have transcribed (see Coates 1987, where I analyse the development of a different topic).

The telling of anecdotes is a common way of introducing a new topic in conversation; sometimes one anecdote is sufficient, sometimes more than one occurs. What characterises these introductory sections, and sets them off from the central development section, is that they are **monologues:** the telling of a story gives the speaker unusual rights to speak. Example 1 below is a transcript of A's introductory anecdote. [*A key for the transcription notation used is given in the Appendix, p. 174.*]

Example 1
A: this bloke I met today who's doing (.) he he's doing some
     postgraduate research at at Stirling (.) anyway I asked him
(3) he he wanted to talk to me about a professional matter and
     I (.) I said (.) I was asking him his sort of background and
(5) he said that he'd done phil<u>os</u>ophy (.) so I was just interested
     with little snippets of philosophy that came my way you see+
(7) and he said one of the things that he was interested in was
     taboo+(.) the nature of taboo+ (.) and he said that (−) and
(9) he gave this example that um (.) if you didn't go to your
     mother's funeral (−) because you'd got something else to do+
(11) (.) it would be very much frowned ⌈upon um even though
                                        D: ⌊oh god =
                                              B: = m

what you had to do could easily be more important+ and
(13) after all she's dead = (.) and wouldn't know you weren't
= C:m
going kind of thing+

Note that A's fellow participants say nothing until the very end
of her narrative. They accord her the right to establish a new
topic – something she doesn't do until the end of her turn – and
it is only when this point is reached that other participants
volunteer supportive noises. No one attempts to make a substantive contribution until it is clear that A has finished her turn.

Once A has finished – and the group has accepted the new
topic – B tells a personal anecdote which illustrates A's general
theme of whether it is taboo to miss your mother's funeral. B's
anecdote is reproduced below.

Example 2

(1) { B: oh we – it's so odd you see because we had this
      ?:   ((xxx))

(2) { B: conversation at dinner tonight =   = because Steve
      A: = mm =

(3) B: MacFadden's mother died at the weekend+ and she

(4) B: [l] (.) well she <u>lived</u> in Brisbane+ ((they were

(5) { B: at Brisbane+)) ⌈so he's going over there+ Australia+
      E: ⌊what (−) Australia?

(6) { B: so he's going to the funeral+ it's obviously
      D: oh my god

(7) { B: gonna cost him a fortune+ (.) and John said
      E: fortune+ (whispers)

(8) { B: (−)   ((he was)) just astonished+ I said
      E: ((s' about £400))

(9) B: (.) well I wouldn't go Steve+ (−) and the and the

(10) { B: [həʊ] as you say it was just taboo+ I mean as far
       C: mm

(11) { B: as ⌈Steve was concerned I mean that was ⌈just
        C: ⌊mm   │
        D: ⌊you just

(12) { B: no+ and I [s] and my response I
       D: can't say that+
       ?:   no+

(13) { B: must "oh John" (−) but sorry ((xxx)) ⌈it's so
       ?:   ((xxx))   │
       C: ⌊I didn't

(14) { B: odd that you should
       C: go over for my father. . . .

While B's right to hold the floor is never challenged, the other participants are far more active than they were during A's narrative. They support her with well placed minimal responses (lines 2, 6, 10, 11, 12), they complete her utterances either at the same time as her ('fortune', line 7) or by briefly taking over from her ('you just can't say that', lines 11–12), they ask for clarification ('what – Australia?', line 5). None of these contributions constitutes an attempt to take the floor from B – they are signals of active listenership.

B's final comment is unfinished as C starts at a point which she interprets as the end of B's turn (though co-participants were clear what B intended to say, namely, that it was a coincidence that A should bring up this subject when she herself had been discussing it that evening in relation to her neighbour). Clearly, the members of the group now feel they have established what topic is under discussion. Thus, C is granted the normal monologue rights when she begins *her* personal anecdote, but as soon as she reaches her first punch line, other speakers intervene and the discussion section begins.

Discussion section, where speakers evaluate the topic, are multiparty in nature. Often several speakers speak at once, and speaker turns tend to be brief. Example 3 below gives C's anecdote and the opening of the general discussion.

Example 3

(1) ⎰ C: I didn't go over for my father+ I asked my mother
    ⎱ B: it's so odd that you should

(2)   C: if she wanted me I mean (.) I I immediately said

(3)   C: "Do you want me to come over?" (−) and she said

(4)   C: "Well no I can't really see the point+ he's dead

(5) ⎧ C: isn't he+ (laughs)   (.) and (.)   ⎡and she
    ⎨ A: mm   │
    ⎩ B: well that's right+ ⎣that's

(6) ⎧ C: said no I mean   ((xxx))   ⎡no point in
    ⎨ B: what John was saying (.) that they   │
    ⎩ E: ⎣you've got

(7) ⎧ C: coming+   so   ⎡
    ⎨ E: terribly forward-looking parents you ⎡see+ it
    ⎩ A: ⎣yeah

(8) ⎰ C:
    ⎱ E: depends on the attitude of (.) mean is is his

(9) ⎧ C: ⎡I don't
    ⎨ E: father still alive?   ⎣because
    ⎩ B: (pp) I don't know+

(10) ⎰ C: think I don't think they had a funeral either+
     ⎱ E: that would have a very big bearing on it+

(11) ⎧ C:
     ⎪ E: ⎡ yeah+
     ⎨ D: if they were religious I mean+ yes   ⎣ it would all

(12) ⎧ C: yeah I don't think they had a funeral+ (.)
     ⎪ E: yeah+ (.) I mean ⎡ if there was if there
     ⎨ D: depend+   ⎣ if there were life

(13) ⎧ C: they had a memorial service+
     ⎪ E: was   ⎡ if they if
     ⎨ D: after death   ⎣ then they'd <u>know</u>

(14) ⎧ C:
     ⎪ E: that's right ((xx))
     ⎩ D: that you hadn't come+

Discussion sections are complex. At one level, individual speakers are dealing with their own feelings about the topic under discussion. In the funeral episode, C keeps returning to the theme of missing her father's funeral, expanding on the reasons for this, and hypothesising that she would go now. A says that she would be upset if her brothers and sister failed to come to her mother's funeral (and since her sister, like C's father, lives in the United States, A is implicitly challenging the assumption that the Atlantic is an insuperable barrier). E, whose parents live in Sheffield, asserts that she would definitely go to their funerals and that it is unthinkable that she wouldn't. These speakers are in effect asking for support from the group, even though their positions are to some extent mutually exclusive; they need to air their feelings in order to deal with them.

At another level, speakers are debating more general points: is it the purpose of funerals to comfort surviving relatives? or are they a public statement about one's feelings for one's dead mother? How important is distance in the decision about whether or not to attend a funeral? The general and personal are intertwined; crucially, speakers work together to sort out what they feel.

From an analytical point of view, the taken-for-granted view of conversation (originating in Sacks, Schegloff & Jefferson 1974) as interaction where one speaker speaks at a time is of little use when dealing with such material. As Example 3 illustrates, more than one speaker speaks at a time: C continues her account of not attending her father's funeral, while B ties this in with her anecdote and E adds a comment about C's parents, responding both to C ('you' in line 6 refers to C) and to B ('is his father still alive?' (lines 8 and 9) is addressed to B – 'his' refers to B's neighbour Steve). E's comment ('that would have a very big bearing on it' at line 10) coincides with C providing further information to fit E's description of her parents as 'forward-looking'. The link between having or not having a funeral service and religious belief is picked up, slightly tongue-in-cheek, by D; E joins in with D, while C continues to refine her account.

The discussion section is long and there isn't space to give it in full nor to analyse it in detail here: specific aspects relating to minimal responses, simultaneous speech and epistemic modality will be picked up in the following three sections (4.2, 4.3 and 4.4). Example 4 gives the end of the discussion, with D's summary and A's final comment.

Example 4

(1) C: I probably I mean it would have also would have

(2) C: been if (.) I'd go now+ (−) Daniel was sort of

(3) ⎰ C: (.) 18 months old+ and it would have been rather
     ⎱ A: mm ....

(4) ⎧ C: difficult and this kind of thing =
     ⎨ A: yes+   yes+
     ⎩ D: = that's right+

(5) ⎰ C: um   I think I
     ⎱ D: I suppose there's two things+ there's

(6) C: would go now because probably because I would want

(7) ⎧ C: to go =   = cos it would be be very easy to go =
     ⎨ E: = mm =
     ⎩ D: = yeah =

(8) ⎧ C: = it would have been (−) I don't know (−)
     ⎨ A: = yeah =
     ⎩ D: there's **two**

(9) ⎰ C: anyway ((xx perfectly all-
     ⎱ D: things aren't there+ there's the the other people

(10) ⎰ C: right xx))
     ⎱ D: like your mother or father who's left and or or

(11) D: siblings+ and there's also how how you feel at that

(12) ⎧ D: time about (.) the easiness of going+
     ⎪ E: mm
     ⎨ C: mm
     ⎪ A: mm
     ⎩ B: yeah

(13) ⎰ D: I mean I would I
     ⎱ A: well to go to Australia seems a

(14) A: bit over the top+

It seems that the group jointly senses that this topic has been satisfactorily dealt with: C receives lots of support in her final statement that she *would* go now since circumstances have changed. Note that D has to make two attempts to provide a summary, starting once before C has finished. C's last turn gets two *yeah*s in sequence (lines 7 and 8). D's summary, like A's initial anecdote, is notable for *lack* of interruption: only when she has completed it do the others respond, all four co-participants indicating, in a perfectly timed sequence of *mm* and *yeah*, their acceptance of what D has said. A, who initiated the topic, then has the last word.

This brief account of the development of one topic in a conversation between women friends provides an example of the way that women develop topics progressively. These women work together to produce the funeral episode, both by recognising opening and closing moves (i.e. granting one speaker the right to initiate a topic through the telling of an anecdote, or to summarise at the end), and by jointly negotiating an understanding of the problem in question (is it taboo to miss your mother's funeral?). This latter part of joint production involves both the right to speak and the duty to listen and support. The five speakers deal with their own and each other's feelings and experiences, juggling speaker and listener roles with great skill. There is no sense in which it is possible to sum up the funeral topic by saying 'A talked about taboo and funerals' or 'C talked about not going to her father's funeral'. The funeral episode is jointly produced by all speakers.

Aries' claim that topics can last up to half an hour is not apparently borne out by this example (which lasts 4 mins 29 secs), but this may depend on the definition of 'topic'. Certainly, topic shift is normally gradual rather than abrupt as the following example demonstrates (Example 5 follows on from Example 4).

Example 5
(1) { A: a bit over the top =
    { E: = yeah what what did the oh yeah
(2) { A: ⌈((xxx he
    { E: what was your bloke saying about taboo?
    { D: ⌊oh yeah
(3) { A: just xxx))
    { D: what? I've just written my *chap*ter on taboo so I'm
(4) { A: well   = I didn't get much more from
    { D: terribly interested =

(5) A: him than that+ except um (.) he's looking at (.)
(6) A: er [ba] battering and his sort of thesis is and
(7) A: the way social services deal with these kind of
(8) A: problems (.) men that batter women (.) and men that
(9) A: (.) sexually abuse their children and um their (.)
(10) A: other children+ and he was just looking at (.)
(11) A: attitudes to that and he said that he's come across
(12) A: incredible taboo (.) taboos um [jə] you know this
(13) A: just world hypothesis (.) business

Note how E's question refers back to A's original anecdote (see Example 1), thus providing a very cohesive link.

In fact, this kind of gradual topic shift continues for many topics:

funerals
↓
child abuse
↓
wives' loyalty to husbands
↓
Yorkshire Ripper
↓
fear of men

These five topics are smoothly linked and overall they last for 15 minutes. 54 seconds. Perhaps Aries' figure more appropriately refers to coherent sequences of topics such as the above. At all events, my data suggest that women do build progressively on each others' contributions, that topics are developed jointly, and that shifts between topics are gradual rather than abrupt.[3]

4.2 Minimal responses

Research on the use of minimal responses is unanimous in showing that women use them more than men (Strodtbeck & Mann 1956; Hirschmann 1974; Zimmerman & West 1975; Fishman 1980). This research is, however, mainly concerned with **mixed** interaction; the finding that women use minimal responses more frequently, and with greater linguistic sensitivity, in such contexts is said to demonstrate yet again the fact that women do the 'interactional shitwork' (to use Fishman's 1977 term).

It shouldn't be automatically assumed that the use of these forms denotes powerlessness, however. The same form functions in different ways in different contexts (see Cameron, McAlinden & O'Leary, Ch. 7 above). Certainly it is clear from my data that the use of minimal responses also characterises linguistic inter-action between women who are friends and equals.

Minimal responses are used in two different ways in the women's conversations I recorded. In the interaction-focussed discussion sections, they are used to support the speaker and to indicate the listener's active attention. The opening of Example 4 (the end of the funeral discussion section) illustrates this. While C talks, first A (lines 3 and 4), then E (line 7), then D and A one after the other (lines 7 and 8) add their minimal responses. These responses are well placed: they are mostly timed to come at the end of an information unit (e.g. a tone group or clause), yet so well anticipated is this point that the speaker's flow is not interrupted. (Both Zimmerman & West and Fishman have shown how the *delayed* minimal response is used by male speakers to indicate lack of interest and/or attention.) These minimal responses signal the listeners' active participation in the conversation; that is, they are another aspect of the way text is *jointly* produced.

In the narrative or more information-focussed sections of the conversation, minimal responses seem to have another meaning. They are used far less frequently, and when they occur they signal agreement among participants that a particular stage of conversation has been reached. For example, when a speaker introduces a new topic, as in Example 1, it is only at the very end that other speakers indicate that they are attending. At this point it seems that D, B and C (lines 11 and 13, Example 1) are indicating to A that they have taken the point of her anecdote, and that they accept it as a topic.

In Example 4, D's summary is followed by minimal responses from all the other participants (line 12). Clearly the women feel the need to indicate their active agreement with D's summing-up. In both these examples, it is not just the presence of minimal responses at the end, but also their absence during the course of an anecdote or summary, which demonstrates the sensitivity of participants to the norms of interaction: speakers recognise different types of talk and use minimal responses appropriately.

So, while it is true to say that the use of minimal responses characterises women's speech in both mixed and single-sex conversation, it would be wrong to claim that you have only to say *mhm* or *yeah* every two minutes to talk like a woman. On the contrary, women's use of minimal responses demonstrates their sensitivity to interactional processes; they use them where they are appropriate. In mixed conversations, the use of minimal responses by women will only become 'weak' where women's skill as listeners is exploited by male speakers. In all-female groups, it seems that the use of these linguistic forms is further evidence of women's active participation in the joint production of text.

4.3 Simultaneous speech

The Sacks, Schegloff and Jefferson (1974) model of turn-taking in conversation views simultaneous speech by two or more co-conversationalists as an aberration. Their model assumes a norm of one speaker speaking at a time. The evidence of my data is that, on the contrary, for much of the time (typically in discussion sections) more than one speaker speaks at a time. The same phenomenon has been observed by Edelsky (1981) and Tannen (1984), both of whom analysed mixed conversation. Edelsky's analysis of five staff meetings reveals what she describes as two types of 'floor': F1, where one speaker dominates, and F2, where several speakers speak at once to jointly produce text. Tannen's analysis of a Thanksgiving dinner involving six speakers (two women, four men) describes two kinds of talk, one more information-focussed, the other more interaction-focussed: the latter involves more than one speaker speaking at the same time.

It is certainly not the case in the conversations I have recorded that where more than one speaker speaks this normally represents an attempt to infringe the current speaker's right to

TABLE 8.1   Simultaneous speech in the funeral episode (4 mins 29 secs)

Type I.	Two speakers self-select at the same time, one stops	3
Type II.	Speaker B self-selects at TRP, A carries on, B stops	3
Type III.	Speaker B self-selects at TRP, A tails off	3
Type IV.	Speaker B completes A's utterance	5
Type V.	Speaker B asks question or comments while A is speaking	7
Type VI.	Speaker B comments, A stops speaking	2
Type VII.	Two speakers speak at the same time	7
		30

(TRP = Transition Relevance Place, i.e. the end of a 'unit type' such as a phrase or clause. See Sacks, Schegloff and Jefferson 1974.)

a turn. I have analysed all instances of simultaneous speech which occur during the funeral episode; only a minority can be described in this way (see Table 8.1).

Type I, where more than one speaker starts at the same time, is trivial: where next speaker self-selects, such infelicities are inevitable. Types II and III are more serious: they are illustrated in Examples 6 and 7 below. In Example 6, E's interruption fails and B completes her own utterance: in Example 7, B stops talking and C claims the floor.

Example 6

(1) { B: I mean ⎡ it's not as if I'm particularly religious+
      { E: ⎣ but if

(2) { B:
      { E: yeah+ but I know but if you've got a [fɑ:] if

(3) { B:
      { E: there's a spouse. . . .

Example 7

(1) { B: but sorry ((xxx)) ⎡ it's so odd that you should
      { C: ⎣ I didn't go over for my father+
      { sev: ((xxx))

(2) { B:
      { C: I asked my mother if she wanted me. . . .

Even with these two examples, the term 'interruption' seems inappropriate. In Example 6, speaker E is guilty of what Tannen calls the 'overlap-as-enthusiasm' strategy: she is not so much trying to stop B from talking as jumping in too soon because of her enthusiasm to participate. She realises her mistake and comes in again once B has finished. (Another example of this phenomenon can be seen in Example 5 where D's enthusiasm delays the start of A's turn.) In Example 7, C assumes that B has finished, and in fact B is one of those speakers, like D (see Example 4, line 13) who typically tail off rather than finishing their turns crisply. It could be argued that B and D's personal style results from their expectation that others know what they mean (so they don't need to say it in full), and that they invite overlap by their habit of ending their turns with utterances which peter out, both syntactically and prosodically. An example of such tailing-off is given below:

Example 8

E: but if there's no spouse I mean **and there's very few relatives left it doesn't really seem much of a** (bold print = laughter)

In Example 8, E's contribution is not overlapped: this example therefore illustrates more starkly how such tailing-off turns are not 'unfinished', in the sense that E has made her contribution and her co-participants know what she means. (To get the full quality of this utterance, it is of course necessary to hear the tape.)

Type IV simultaneous speech is closely related to the above: if a speaker tails off, then it is open to other participants to complete the utterance. Speaker B's habit of not completing her turn often results in others (usually E) doing it for her:

Example 9
(1) B: I just thought "if the car breaks down on the way
(2) B: home I mean I'll die of fear+ (laughs) I'll never
(3) ⎰ B: get out+ I'll just" (.)
    ⎱ E: just sit here and die+

In this case there is no overlap, but often speakers' completion of each others' utterances results in simultaneous speech:

Example 10
⎰ B: I mean that⎡was just   = no+
⎱ D: ⎣you just can't say that =

Note that B acknowledges D's contribution and in fact continues speaking: D's overlap in no way constitutes an attempt to get the floor.

Such completion-overlaps can involve more than two speakers:

Example 11
(1) ⎧ A: it'll become a [s] public statement about =
    ⎨ E: = the
    ⎩ D:
(2) ⎧ A: er   ((xx))   yeah+
    ⎨ E: family+ ((to do with)) you
    ⎩ D: yeah+   and that you're close+

Again, as in Example 10, the current speaker (A) acknowledges the others' contributions before continuing.

Type V is a very common type of simultaneous speech: it involves one of the co-participants asking the speaker a question, or commenting on what the speaker is saying, during the speaker's turn. One could describe this phenomenon as a relation of the minimal response: the questions or comments function as a sign of active listenership, and do not threaten current speaker's turn. Speakers in fact acknowledge such questions/comments while continuing to hold the floor. Examples 12 and 13 illustrate the question, where listeners seek clarification.

Example 12
(1) { B: well she lived in Brisbane+ ((they were at
     { E:
(2) { B   Brisbane+)) | so he's going over there+ Australia+
     { E: ⌈ what (−)   Australia?
(3) { B: so he's going to the funeral+
     { E:

Example 13
(1) { A: and I imagine that my two far-flung sibs will
     { E:
(2) { A: actually make the journey+   ⌈ I'm just (.) I'm
     { E: ⌊ what (.) to your
(3) { A: ((almost)) yes I'm sure they will but it'll be
     { E: parents?   to your mother's?
(4) { A: because [ɪ] it'll become a [s] public statement. . . .
     { E:

In Example 12, B tucks 'Australia' into her exposition to satisfy E, while A, in 13, interrupts herself to say 'yes' to E before continuing her statement about her sister and brother.

Comments occur more frequently than questions and normally don't threaten a speaker's turn:

Example 14
  { A: I'm absolutely sure they'll come but I mean in fact it
  { E:
  { A: won't make any odds but I think I (.) would be (.) hurt
  { E: it'll be nicer for
  { A: and angry if they hadn't+
  { E: you+

In this example, E's comment goes unacknowledged, but speakers often do respond to listener comments:

Example 15
(1) { E: if there's a spouse then perhaps they <u>would</u> want
     { A:

(2) $\left\{\begin{array}{l} \text{E:} \\ \text{A:} \end{array}\right.$
     E: you to go   you know but if   but if   = that's
     A: yeah for their comfort+ for them =

(3) $\left\{\begin{array}{l} \text{E:} \\ \text{A:} \end{array}\right.$
     E: right+ comfort for them+ but if. . .
     A:

Here E acknowledges A's comment before continuing.

Occasionally comments of this kind coincide with the current speaker stopping speaking (Type VI). In the following example, C finishes making her point during E's comment about her parents, and it is E who then takes the floor. C's *so* is ambiguous: it could be a bid for a longer turn (which fails), or it could be a tailing-off noise.

Example 16

(1) $\left\{\begin{array}{l} \text{C:} \\ \text{E:} \end{array}\right.$
     C: and she said "no" I mean ((xx))   ⌈no point in coming+
     E: ⌊you've got terribly

(2) $\left\{\begin{array}{l} \text{C:} \\ \text{E:} \end{array}\right.$
     C: so
     E: forward-looking parents you see+ it depends on the

(3) $\left\{\begin{array}{l} \text{C:} \\ \text{E:} \end{array}\right.$
     C:
     E: attitude. . .

This example is complicated by the fact that B is also talking at the same time (see example 3, lines 5–9 for the full version). However such an example is categorised, what is important is that E's contribution here is constructive: she is embellishing C's turn, putting C's mother's behaviour in context.

The final type of simultaneous speech, type VII, involves two or more speakers speaking at once; for this type it is not possible to say one speaker has the floor and the other is merely interjecting a comment. There are seven examples of this during the funeral episode (i.e. nearly a quarter of all examples of simultaneous speech). The obvious analogy is again a musical one: the speakers contribute simultaneously to the same theme, like several instruments playing contrapuntally (the notion of contrapuntal talk is also invoked in Reisman 1974). Examples 17 and 18 below illustrate this type:

Example 17

(1) $\left\{\begin{array}{l} \text{E:} \\ \text{B:} \\ \text{C:} \end{array}\right.$
     E: is his father still alive?   because that
     B: (pp) I don't know
     C: I don't think

(2) $\left\{\begin{array}{l} \text{E:} \\ \text{C:} \end{array}\right.$
     E: would have a very big bearing on it+
     C: they had a funeral either+

Example 18

(1) { A: I've [bp] for many years ((have wondered)) about my
    { E: cos that's what funerals are for
(2) { A: own (mother's funeral+
    { E: (.) they're for the relatives+

Without providing an audio-tape, it is hard to describe the
quality of such passages: crucially, there is no sense of competition, or of vying for turns. Speakers do not become aggrieved
when others join in. The feel of the conversation is that all the
participants are familiar with each other and with the way the
interaction is constructed. It is very much a joint effort, with
individual speakers concerned to contribute to a jointly negotiated whole.

A final more extended example, containing four instances of
simultaneous speech, will serve to give the flavour of the conversation as a whole.

Example 19

(1) C: I mean I think it really depends on the <u>attitude</u> of
(2) { C: the survivors who are ⎡ there+ (−) if if they want
    { B: ⎣ yeah+
(3) { C: the person to ⎡ go   (−) then the person should go+
    { E: ⎣ mm+
    { A: I don't think it depends on that
(4) { C:
    { E: ⎡ oh I do+ if one of
    { A: Cathy+ I think it depends on ⎣ um
(5) { C:
    { E: mine died and (.) er I mean (−) my (.) if it were
(6) { C:
    { E: whichever one it were the other one would expect me
(7) { C:
    { E: to go (−) they'd be <u>absolutely</u> <u>staggered</u> if I
(8) { C:
    { E: didn't (−) ⎡ especially as it's only (.) (laughs) two
    { D: ⎣ mm
(9) { C: = no I mean if my mother had wanted
    { E: hours away+
    { D: Sheffield = (laughs)
(10){ C: me to come+ if she'd said "oh yes please" (.) ⎡ or
    { A: mm   ⎢
    { E: ⎣ you

(11) C: "of course" or or something+   then I would've
     A: yeah+
     E: would've gone+
(12) C: (.) of course I would've gone+
     A: yeah+

At the beginning of Example 19, A's conflicting point of view overlaps with C's talking (note that C completes her utterance) and E's support for C overlaps with A, who tails off. That an interpretation of this as conflict is false is shown by A's support (given in minimal responses) for C's restatement of her point of view at the end. The contrapuntal nature of such text is exemplified by D's contribution 'Sheffield', which glosses E's 'it's only two hours away', and by E's anticipation of C's words which leads her to butt in with 'you would've gone' before C herself says it.

As someone who was a participant in this discourse, there is no doubt in my mind that the term 'interruption' is hardly ever appropriate as a description of instances of simultaneous speech which occur in gossip. In public domains, where the norm is that one speaker speaks at a time, and where the goal of participants is to grab speakership, then interruption is a strategy for gaining the floor. In private conversation between equals, on the other hand, where the chief goal of interaction is the maintenance of good social relationships, then the participation of more than one speaker is iconic of joint activity: the goal is not to take the floor *from* another speaker, but to participate in conversation *with* other speakers. The examples of simultaneous speech given here illustrate the way in which women speakers work together to produce shared meanings.

4.4 Epistemic modality

Epistemic modal forms are defined semantically as those linguistic forms which are used to indicate the speaker's confidence or lack of confidence in the truth of the proposition expressed in the utterance. If someone says *Perhaps she missed the train*, the use of the word *perhaps* indicates lack of confidence in the proposition 'she missed the train'. Lexical items such as *perhaps*, *I think*, *sort of*, *probably*, as well as certain prosodic and paralinguistic features, are used in English to express epistemic modality.

Such forms, however, are used by speakers not just to indicate their lack of commitment to the truth of propositions, but also to hedge assertions in order to protect both their own and addressees' face (for a full account of the role of epistemic modality in spoken discourse, see Coates 1987). It is my impression (based on an admittedly small corpus of data) that women in single-sex groups exploit these forms more than men. Table 8.2 gives the totals for the most commonly used forms in two parallel texts, each lasting about 40 minutes.[4]

TABLE 8.2   Sex differences in the use of epistemic modal forms

	Women	Men
I mean	77	20
well	65	45
just	57	48
I think	36	12
sort of	35	10

Utterances such as those in Examples 20 and 21 below are typical of the discussion sections of the all-women conversations recorded (epistemic modal forms in italics).

Example 20
[funeral discussion]
I mean I think it *really* depends on the <u>attitude</u> of the survivors who are 'there+

Example 21
[speaker describes old friend she'd recently bumped into]
she looks very *sort of* um (−) *kind of* matronly *really*+

It is my contention (see Coates 1987: 129) that women exploit the polypragmatic nature of epistemic modal forms. They use them to mitigate the force of an utterance in order to respect addressees' face needs. Thus, the italicised forms in Example 21 hedge the assertion *she looks matronly* not because the speaker doubts its truth but because she does not want to offend her addressees by assuming their agreement (describing a friend in unflattering terms is controversial). Such forms also protect the speaker's face: the speaker in Example 21 can retreat from the proposition expressed there if it turns out to be unacceptable. Where sensitive topics are discussed (as in Examples 20 and 21), epistemic modal forms are used frequently. This seems to provide an explanation for women's greater use of such forms (see Table

8.2). The women's conversations I have analysed involve topics related to people and feelings (see, for example, the topic sequence given in 4.1, page 105); in the parallel all-male conversation I have analysed, the men talk about *things* – home beer-making, hi-fi systems, etc. Presumably such topics do not trigger the use of epistemic modal forms because they are not so face-threatening.

Women also use these forms to facilitate open discussion (and, as I've said, epistemic modal forms are mostly found in the discussion sections of conversation). An underlying rule of conversation between equals, where the exchange of information is not a priority, is 'Don't come into open disagreement with other participants' (see Leech 1983: 132). Examples 20 and 21 are contributions to discussion which state a point of view but allow for other points of view. More positively, epistemic modal forms can be used to invite others to speak, a function often fulfilled by the tag question.

As Perkins (1983: 111) says: 'since questions qualify the truth of a proposition by making it relative to the speaker's uncertainty, they may be regarded as expressing epistemic modality'. An analysis of the tag questions used in the conversations I have recorded shows that the vast majority are addressee-oriented rather than speaker-oriented (cf. Holmes, 1984; Cameron, McAlinden & O'Lary, Ch. 7 above). In one of the conversations (about 40 minutes of taped material) there are 23 tag questions, yet of these only four are used to elicit information (i.e. only four are speaker-oriented), as in Example 22:

Example 22
you don't know what colour their bluè is dó you (Note the rising intonation contour on the tag.)

Addressee-oriented tags can be used either to soften the force of a negatively affective utterance, or to facilitate interaction. Of the 19 addressee-oriented tags in the conversation, only one functions as a softener; the rest are all facilitative. Facilitative tags are given this name precisely because they are used to facilitate the participation of others; they invite them into the discourse. The following examples illustrate this (tags are italicised):

Example 23
{ E: but I mean so much research is male-dominated+ I mean
{ A:
{ E: it's just stàggering *isn't it* =
{ A: = mm+

Example 24

{ D: it was dreàdful *wàsn't it* =
{ E: = appalling Caroline

{ D:
{ E: absolutely appalling+

What is surprising about the tag questions in my data is that, while I would argue that they are facilitative, they are mostly not found in contexts like Examples 23 and 24, that is, where the tag results in another speaker taking a turn. Instead, they occur in mid-utterance, and the speaker seems to expect no verbal response (or at most a minimal response). Examples 25 and 26 illustrate this type:

Example 25

I think the most difficult thing is is that when you love someone you you half the time you forget their faults (yes) *don't you* and still maybe love them but I mean . . .

Example 26

[Discussion of Yorkshire Ripper case]

{ A: and they had they had a very accurate picture of him
{ D:

{ A: *dìdn't they*+ they roughly knew his age =
{ D: = at one point

{ A: = yeah =
{ D: they knew about his gap teeth too *didn't they* =

{ A:
{ D: = then they got rid of that+

A further example is given in Example 4 (page 103), where D's summary at the end of the funeral discussion begins *there's twò things àren't there*. Of the 18 facilitative tags, nine occur in mid-utterance, like these; another three come at the end of a speaker's turn but elicit no overt response – for example, during the funeral discussion, E comments on the theme of missing a funeral *it's just not gòing ìsn't it*. Most of the other facilitative tags appear as comments by active listeners (Type V simultaneous speech) as in Example 27:

Example 27

{ D: cos I'm fed up of travelling to conferences[but I'm
{ B: [oh it's so

{ D: giving a paper.
{ B: tỳpical *ìsn't it*

All these examples involve falling intonation, and all expect the answer *yes* (like *nonne* in Latin).

The women conversationalists seem to use these tags to check the taken-for-grantedness of what is being said. Paralinguistic cues, and sometimes minimal responses, signal to the speaker that what she is saying has the support of the group. Confirmation of this interpretation còmes from an example where the speaker does not receive the expected response:

Example 28
```
    A:   what I can't fathom out is why children who are
    A:   physically battered by their parents (.) there's no,
    A:   there's never any suggestion that (.) they contributed
  ⌠ A:   to it (.) and yet children who are sexually abused by
  ⌡ E:           yes there is
    A:   their parents (.) somehow that's (−) you know the [tʃɪ]
  ⌠ A:   the the
  ⌡ E:   well there is (−) because there's that thing of a
  ⌠ A:
  ⎱ E:   certain pitch of scrèaming *isn't there* =
  ⌡ C:                                              = ah but no
  ⌠ A:
  ⎱ E:                              ⌠ oh      = sorry =
  ⌡ C:   that's logical+            ⎱ genuine =         = she's um she's talking
  ⌠ A:
  ⎱ E:                     oh
  ⌡ C:   about the emotional ((sort of)) feeling+
```

E's *oh sorry* demonstrates her surprise and also the fact that speakers in this type of discourse are prepared to withdraw statements which turn out *not* to be accepted by others present.

I want to argue that these tags are not only addressee-oriented, in the normal sense of 'facilitative', but that they also function, sometimes simultaneously, to mark the speaker's monitoring of the progress of the conversation. This may involve the establishment and development of new topics. The following example is taken from the point in the conversation where the topic shifts from child abuse to wives' loyalty to husbands.

Example 29

C: and your husband has become a monster =
A: = mm
B: = mm (.)
C: ‖ *[end of child*
A: ‖ *abuse topic]*
B: mm (.)   ‖
E: ‖ I mean it's like that woman who turned in (.)
E: was it (.) [pr] Prime . . . one of those spy cases+ it
E: was his wife *wàsn't it* who turned him in =
A: = yeah+
D: = oh yes+

E's tag question here serves to get agreement from the group to pursue a new aspect of the topic; it functions as a *check* on the co-operative progress of the discourse.

5. Co-operativeness

In some senses, co-operativeness is a taken-for-granted feature of conversation: Grice, in his well known analysis of conversational norms (Grice 1975), used the term 'co-operative' to underscore the obvious but often overlooked fact that conversations can only occur because two or more participants tacitly agree to co-operate in talk. The notion of co-operativeness that has become established in the literature on women's language, however, (see, for example, Kalcik 1975; Aries 1976; Goodwin 1980; Maltz & Borker 1982), is less general: co-operativeness in this sense refers to a particular *type* of conversation, conversation where speakers work together to produce shared meanings. Set against this notion of co-operativeness is the notion of competitiveness; competitiveness is used to describe the adversarial style of conversation where speakers vie for turns and where participants are more likely to contradict each other than to build on each others' contributions. (Whether competitiveness in this sense is typical of all-male discourse is a folklinguistic myth which has still to be tested.)

At the heart of co-operativeness is a view of speakers collaborating in the production of text: the group takes precedence over the individual. How far does my data support the idea that women's language is co-operative in this more specific sense? Do the formal features described in the previous section function as collaborative devices?

At one level, we have seen that topics develop slowly and

accretively because participants build on each others' contributions and jointly arrive at a consensus. At a more delicate level, both minimal responses and epistemic modal forms function as enabling devices. Participants use minimal responses to signal their active listenership and support for the current speaker; they use them too to mark their recognition of the different stages of conversational development. Epistemic modal forms are used to respect the face needs of all participants, to negotiate sensitive topics, and to encourage the participation of others; the chief effect of using epistemic modal forms is that the speaker does not take a hard line. Where a group rather than an individual overview is the aim of discussion, then linguistic forms which mitigate the force of individual contributions are a valuable resource. Finally, simultaneous speech occurs in such discourse in various forms, and is rarely a sign of conversational malfunctioning. On the contrary, in much of the material I have collected, the norm of one-speaker-at-a-time clearly does not apply. Co-conversationalists ask questions or make comments which, like minimal responses, are signals of active listenership, but which more substantially help to produce joint text. Simultaneous speech also occurs when speakers complete each others' utterances: this seems to be a clear example of the primacy of text rather than speaker. Finally, simultaneous speech occurs most commonly because speakers prefer, in discussion, the affirmation of collaborative talk to the giving of the floor to one speaker. Participants in conversation can absorb more than one message at a time; simultaneous speech doesn't threaten comprehension. On the contrary, it allows for a more multilayered development of themes.

Topic development, minimal responses, epistemic modal forms and simultaneous speech are formal features of very different kinds. Yet where minimal responses and epistemic modal forms are used frequently and with sensitivity, where simultaneous speech is contrapuntal and doesn't mark conversational breakdown, and where topics develop slowly and progressively, all can be seen to function to promote co-operative talk. It seems that in conversations between women friends in an informal context, the notion of co-operativeness is not a myth.

6. Conclusions

In this chapter I have tried to refine Jones's description of gossip, in particular by analysing some of the formal features which characterise all-female discourse. A comprehensive account of the formal features typical of gossip remains to be carried out. But it is possible on the basis of the four features analysed here to conclude that women's talk *can* be described as co-operative. This, however, brings us up against the conflicting findings of those working on women's language in the context of *mixed* interaction. Women's use of minimal responses, tag questions, and hedging devices in general (epistemic modal forms) has been interpreted as a sign of weakness, of women's subordinate position to men (see, for example, Lakoff 1975; Fishman 1977, 1980). Moreover, research on interruption and overlap in mixed and single-sex pairs has shown that men use interruptions to dominate conversation in mixed interaction, but that simultaneous speech of any kind is rare in single sex conversation (Zimmerman & West 1975; West & Zimmerman 1983).

Firstly, it is clearly not the case that any one linguistic form has one single function irrespective of contextual factors; linguists are now aware that linguistic forms are potentially multifunctional (see Cameron, McAlinden and O'Leary, Ch. 7, for a full discussion of this point). Secondly, as I argued in section 3, the forms that characterise all-female discourse need to be understood in the framework of the goals they serve. Since it is the aim of such talk to create and maintain good social relationships, then forms which promote such ends will be preferred. I have tried to show that women's frequent use of minimal responses and epistemic modal forms, their way of developing topics progressively, and their preference for all-together-now rather than one-at-a-time discussion, all serve the function of asserting joint activity and of consolidating friendship. Women's talk at one level deals with the experiences common to women: individuals work to come to terms with that experience, and participants in conversation actively support one another in that endeavour. At another level, the *way* women negotiate talk symbolises that mutual support and co-operation: conversationalists understand that they have rights as speakers and also duties as listeners; the joint working out of a group point of view takes precedence over individual assertions.

This discussion of underlying goals should help to explain the differences between language use in same-sex and mixed interaction. It is undoubtedly the case, all other things being equal, that when women interact with other women they interact with equals, while when they interact with men they are relating to superiors. This means that analysis of mixed interaction has to be conducted in a framework which acknowledges dominance and oppression as relevant categories. Giving a minimal response to an equal in conversation, for example, is very different from giving a minimal response to a superior. Where the main goal of relaxed informal conversation between equals is the maintenance of good (equal) social relationships, one of the goals of mixed interaction is inevitably the maintenance of gender divisions, of male–female inequality.

Furthermore, it is now agreed that sociocultural presuppositions are a key factor in explaining how speakers make sense of conversation (Gumperz 1982a). Since it is arguable that women and men in our culture do not share these sociocultural presuppositions, then another difference between same-sex and mixed interaction will be that the latter will exhibit communication problems similar to those found in inter-ethnic conversation.

For both these reasons, it is very important that we do not conflate the 'women's language' said to be typical of mixed interaction with the 'women's language' which characterises all-female discourse. The two need to be analysed separately. However, growing awareness of the norms of all-female discourse may help us to reassess our interpretation of the linguistic forms used by women in mixed interaction.

Jones's original paper marked the beginning of an important shift in focus in work on language and sex differences. It drew attention not just to women's language *per se*, but to the *strengths* of such discourse. This positive approach has provided an important counterbalance to the more negative tone of researchers who see women's language as weak and tentative. Much remains to be done in the study of women and language: the majority of studies so far have concentrated on white educated women in the United States and Britain. We still know very little about variation in women's language relating to age or class or ethnic group. The notion of co-operativeness needs to be tested against all these parameters. Jones's argument is that, despite differences of age or class or ethnicity, women form a speech community. In so far as human interaction is constitutive of social reality, and in so far as interaction with other women plays an important role in our dealing with our experiences as women, then the study of interaction in all-woman groups is, as Jones says, 'a key to the female subculture'.

Notes

1. I describe, and give a justification of, this approach in greater detail in Coates (1987).

2. I would like to place on record my gratitude to my friends for their tolerance and support.

3. Abrupt shifts do occur, when the emphasis switches from interaction-focussed to more information-focussed episodes. Such shifts, however, form a minority of cases.

4. The two texts used were one of my own, and one from the Survey of English Usage (University College, London). The speakers in both were white, middle-class, well educated, aged in their 30s and early 40s. Both texts were recorded in the evening in the homes of linguists who had invited their friends over for a drink. Five women are involved in the first text; three men in the other. (My thanks to Professor Greenbaum for allowing me to use SEU material.)

Chapter 9

Talk control: an illustration from the classroom of problems in analysing male dominance of conversation[1]

Joan Swann

1. Women and men talking

The stereotype of the over-talkative woman stands out in stark contrast to most research studies of interactions between women and men, which argue that, by and large, it is men who tend to dominate the talk. For instance, men have been found to use more interruptions (Zimmerman & West 1975; Eakins & Eakins 1976; West & Zimmerman 1983; West 1984) and simply to talk more than women (e.g. Soskin & John 1963; Bernard 1972; Swacker 1975; Eakins & Eakins 1976). In mixed-sex conversations it has been found that men's topics are more often pursued, while women play a 'supportive' role (Fishman 1978, 1983; see also Hirschman 1974; and Leet-Pellegrini 1980). The picture is not universally one-sided: Beattie (1981), in a study of university tutorials, found that women students interrupted as often as men and Edelsky (1981), looking at university committee meetings, found that women could hold their own in informally organised, 'collaboratively developed', talk, though not in the more formal 'one-person-at-a-time' talk that tends to be prevalent in meetings. In most contexts, however, the evidence remains that men tend to be the dominant parties in mixed-sex conversations and discussions.

Related to these findings is the suggestion that women tend, more often than men, to use a speech style that gives the impression of politeness, tact, hesitancy and uncertainty. One of the best known exponents of this view is Lakoff who suggested that the characteristics of 'women's language' include: 'empty' adjectives such as *divine, charming* and *cute*; question-intonation in statement contexts, e.g.: *'What's your name, dear?'* – *'Mary*

Smith?'; tag questions (a question tagged on to a declarative, of the form *isn't it? wasn't she? don't you?* – e.g. 'It's so hot, isn't it?'); and the use of hedges that might normally indicate uncertainty – e.g. *sort of, kinda, I guess*; (see Lakoff 1975: 53 ff). It's worth noting here that Lakoff's work was based on her intuitions as a member of a North American, educated, White, middle-class community rather than on any formal survey. Some of her claims at least have been contested by other researchers (for instance, tag-questions have been found as frequently in male as in female speech – Baumann (1976); Dubois and Crouch (1975); Cameron, McAlinden and O'Leary, (Ch. 7). For a critique of Lakoff see also Chapter 7 in this book).

Some interpretations of the research mentioned above have focussed on gender differences *per se*. Maltz and Borker (1982), like Lakoff, draw up a list of 'women's features' (such as a greater tendency to ask questions, and to make use of positive minimal responses such as *mhm* or *yeah*, p. 197) and 'men's features' (such as a tendency to interrupt women, p. 198). Maltz and Borker argue that these differences arise because women and men come from different 'sociolinguistic subcultures', have learnt different rules of friendly interaction and interpret the use of certain conversational features differently.

Gender differences in conversation are, however, more commonly interpreted in terms of differences in power between women and men. West and Zimmerman (1977), for instance, note that differential use of interruptions is related not simply to gender but can be found in other asymmetrical talk such as that between parents and children. West and Zimmerman see gender and power as inextricably linked: 'gestures of power [such as interruptions etc.] – minor in import viewed one by one – are an integral part of women's *placement* in the social scheme of things. These daily gestures are constant "reminders" which help constitute women's subordinate status' (1983: 110; authors' italics). In a later study of doctor–patient talk, West (1984) suggests gender may function as a superordinate status, taking primacy over other indicators of power such as professional status.

O'Barr and Atkins (1980) interpret differences in women's and men's speech in terms of power *rather than* of gender. In a study of courtroom discourse they found occurrences of Lakoff's 'women's' features in the speech of both men and women, and suggest that the use of such features is associated with status, and not directly with gender. They argue, therefore, that these features are characteristic of a speaking style that they term 'powerless language'. While they do not dispute that the features of their 'powerless language' may, in many contexts, occur more frequently in the speech of women than of men, they suggest this is due simply to the fact that women tend to occupy less powerful social positions than men.

2. Some problems of interpretation

The argument that certain features of talk are characteristic of female or male speakers, and that the use of such features leads to male dominance of talk in fact poses one or two problems that have both practical (analytical) and theoretical implications.

(i) The first, and most straightforward problem is that of agreeing on a formal definition of conversational features. Interruptions provide one illustration of this. It has been argued (by, for instance, Sacks, Schegloff & Jefferson 1974) that smooth turn exchanges between speakers depend in part upon the existence of 'transition relevance places' – points where a sequence in the current speaker's turn is grammatically complete and at which it might be reasonable for the turn to end, and for the next speaker to begin. Zimmerman and West's (1975) definition of 'interruptions' covered any simultaneous speech that began *before* the word preceding such a 'transition relevance place'.[2] Speaker B's utterance in Example 1 would therefore be classified as an interruption by Zimmerman and West (for transcription conventions, see Appendix, p. 174):

Example 1
A: I don't know what you're talking about OK tell me what
  ⌈it's all about
B: ⌊Just throw a dice just throw a dice

At least one reason why Beattie's (1981) results (mentioned above) may differ from those of Zimmerman and West is that Beattie used different criteria to identify interruptions. Beattie distinguished several different kinds of interruption, but his 'simple interruptions' are closest to Zimmerman and West's 'interruption' category. Beattie's definition of interruption depends upon the notion of 'completeness'. An interruption is said to occur when the current speaker's turn is left incomplete. Completeness is judged intuitively on the basis of verbal and nonverbal cues, but the important thing is that this judgement is made at the point when the first speaker *stops* speaking, rather than where the second speaker *starts*. The example above, therefore, would not be classified as an interruption by Beattie, but Example 2 would:

Example 2
A: . . . so he (.) he gives the impression that he he wasn't able to train them up. ⌈Now
B: ⌊He didn't try hard enough heh heh heh.
(Adapted from Beattie 1983: 115.)

Although I've taken interruptions as an example here, there are similar problems in formally identifying other features (such as questions) and even in measuring the amount of talk produced by different speakers.

(ii) Having made some formal identification of conversation features and found differences between women's and men's use of these, the problem remains of how any differences should be interpreted. One point to make is that such features have been *associated* with the speech of women and men – gender differences are not categorical. Then, these features are associated with women's and men's speech in particular contexts (women have been found to speak less by some researchers in certain contexts; to use more questions by other researchers in other contexts; differential use of interruptions – leaving aside for the moment the problem of identifying these – has been found in some contexts and not in others). Simply aggregating the results of different research studies to determine sets of 'women's' and 'men's' features is, then, problematical.

(iii) There are also difficulties in attaching a meaning or function to particular conversational features. To look again at interruptions, West and Zimmerman (1983: 103) interpret these as 'violations of speakers' turns at talk'. Beattie (1983) concedes that interruptions need not always signal conversational dominance, but still seems to see them as signs of competition for the floor. Kalčik (1975), however, in a study of women's consciousness-raising groups, found many instances of interruption that she claimed functioned as supporters of someone's conversational topic, by finishing off an idea, rather than as take-over bids. Any interpretation of conversational features must actually be highly context-specific. In some circumstances (in a particular type of conversation, between particular people, with a particular goal, etc.) interruptions may be an indicator of conversational dominance; in other circumstances, they may not. This same point will apply to other features, such as the use of questions, minimal responses, etc. Within the contexts they studied I have no doubt researchers such as Fishman and Zimmerman and West made appropriate interpretations of the features they identified, but particular interpretations cannot be considered as fixed attributes of formally identified conversational features.

(iv) Related to the point above is the (by now well established) notion that the same conversational function may be fulfilled by different formally identified features. Dominance or control of talk may be exercised in a variety of ways, both linguistic and nonlinguistic. Any analysis of 'male dominance' of talk should, therefore, take account of a range of different conversational features, of nonverbal behaviour and, ideally, of contextual factors such as seating arrangements, any activities that accompany the talk, etc.

(v) A final point relates to the explanation of gender differences in talk in terms of differences in power between women and men. How is it that women constitute a (relatively) powerless group and are therefore subject to domination by men?

Women have often been regarded as a powerless social group, not just in studies of male/female interaction but also in more general work on the position of women in society. Any such argument seems to me to pose one or two problems. For instance, the argument encompasses several points. It may refer to the fact that *on average* men hold more powerful positions in our society; or alternatively that, all other things being equal, women have less chance than men to occupy a position of authority (to take employment as an example, that women do less well than men with similar qualifications or experience). These inequalities have been well-enough documented (see, for instance, Byrne 1978; Deem 1978; and Delamont 1980, on career patterns and opportunities for women and men in education). While they do fit in with O'Barr and Atkins's explanations of differences between 'women's' and 'men's' speech they do not, however, seem to account for the evidence from other studies mentioned above that, even in the absence of factors such as formal status, men may still in various ways dominate talk, and that gender may on occasion over-ride formal status. I would suggest a slightly different argument here – that both women and men see men as the dominant sex, and so when gender is salient in an interaction (i.e. when it seems relevant to be seen as a woman or a man, rather than as a doctor, lawyer, etc.) men would tend to dominate.

However the notion of male 'dominance' itself is rather problematical. While many studies have shown that men's interests tend to be better served than women's in mixed-sex conversation (as, for instance, in Fishman's 1978 study, where topics initiated by men are more often followed up and pursued), it is likely that both women and men contribute to this state of affairs. In other words, the use of terms such as 'dominate' and 'control' should not suggest that men need linguistically to bludgeon women into submission. Where it is seen as normal that men talk more, etc. they may do so with the complicity of women. This argument would apply also to other asymmetrical relationships such as that between a doctor and a patient or a teacher and a child. When someone's authority is regarded as normal or legitimate it is unlikely that it will be contested. Rather, all parties in an inter-action will contribute to its maintenance.

I'd like now to illustrate some of the points I've just made by looking at examples of classroom talk.

3. Classroom talk: an illustration

Classroom talk is an interesting area of study partly because many educationists argue that talk itself is an important vehicle for learning:

> The way into ideas, the way of making ideas truly one's own, is to be able to think them through, and the best way to do this for most people is to talk them through. Thus talking is not merely a way of conveying existing ideas to others; it is also a way by which we explore ideas, clarify them, and make them our own. Talking things over allows the sorting of ideas, and gives rapid and extensive practice towards the handling of ideas. (Marland 1977: 129)

The classroom is also one place in which children learn social roles. An influential argument is that socially appropriate behav-iour (including gender-appropriate behaviour) is learnt in part (though not by any means exclusively) through classroom talk.

Studies of classroom life have found many ways, linguistic and nonlinguistic, in which girls and boys are treated differently. For instance, pupils are often segregated by gender as an aid to class-room administration, or told to do things as boys or as girls as a form of motivation (girls may be told to leave first very quietly, boys to sing as nicely as the girls); pupils are often told that certain topics are 'boys'' topics or will 'mainly appeal to the girls'; topics are often chosen specifically with a view to main-taining boys' interests; boys insist on, and are given, greater attention by the teacher; in practical subjects such as science boys tend to hog the resources; boys are more disruptive; and boys, in various ways, dominate classroom talk. (See Byrne 1978; Deem 1978; and Delamont 1980, for a general discussion of these and other findings; Whyte 1986, for a report on science teaching; and Clarricoates 1983, for a discussion of classroom interaction.)

Talk may, therefore, be seen to play its part alongside much more general patterns of difference and discrimination. Studies that focus on characteristics of mixed-sex classroom talk produce results that are similar in many respects to the general studies of talk between women and men mentioned above. For instance, in an American study of over 100 classes Sadker and Sadker (1985) found that boys spoke on average three times as much as girls, that boys were eight times more likely than girls to call out answers, and that teachers accepted such answers from boys but reprimanded girls for calling out. French and French (1984) suggest that particular strategies may enable talkative boys to gain more than their fair share of classroom talk. In a study of (British) primary classrooms they found that simply making an unusual response to a teacher's question could gain a pupil extra speaking turns – and those who made such responses were more often boys.

Most studies of classroom talk focus on the role of the teacher as much as on different pupils. One characteristic of classroom talk (that distinguishes it from talk in many other contexts) is that this is often mediated (if not directly controlled) by the teacher. If boys are to dominate, therefore, they must do so with the teacher's assistance or at least tacit acceptance. The argument that teachers pay boys more attention and, in other ways, encourage them to talk more has led some people consciously to attempt to redress the balance. Such evidence as is available, however, suggests that old habits are hard to break. Spender (1982) claims that it is virtually impossible to divide one's attention equally between girls and boys. Whyte (1986) is less pessimistic. Observations of science lessons by researchers involved in the Manchester-based Girls Into Science and Technology project revealed that teachers were able to devote an equal amount of attention to girls and boys, and therefore to encourage more equal participation from pupils. This was only achieved with some effort, however. Whyte reports a head of science who, having managed to create an atmosphere in which girls and boys contributed more or less equally to discussion, remarked that he had felt as though he were devoting 90 per cent of his attention to the girls (1986: 196).

While the fact of male dominance of classroom talk makes this similar to mixed-sex talk in other contexts, it's worth noting that not all of the same indicators of conversational dominance are present. For instance, although the findings that boys act assertively in the classroom (by calling out, etc.) may seem to be in line with the results from some adult 'interruption' studies, I know of no systematic studies (similar to those of Beattie or Zimmerman and West) of the use of interruptions by pupils in classrooms. With regard to minimal responses, one would not expect to find them heavily used by pupils in certain types of classroom talk (such as teacher-led question-and-answer sessions). Question-usage itself is hardly restricted to girl pupils – and questions used by the teacher may function as a form of control rather than as a means of gaining attention or the right to a speaking turn (see for instance D. Edwards 1980). If boys are to attempt to dominate classroom talk (relative to girls), such dominance must fit with the context and with the behaviour of other participants – in this case chiefly the teacher, who is meant to be in control, overall, of what is going on.

I want to discuss some of these issues further in relation to an exploratory study of classroom talk that I carried out with a colleague, and which is described in greater detail elsewhere (see Swann and Graddol 1988).

3.1 An exploratory study of classroom talk

Given imbalances that had been found in earlier work between girls' and boys' participation in classroom talk the intention in this study was to examine in detail:

1. the mechanisms of turn allocation and turn exchange that support male dominance of classroom talk;
2. the roles played by different participants (girls, boys and the class teacher) in the achievement of such interactional dominance.

To do this, we made a close examination of video-recordings of two twenty-minute sequences of small-group teaching with primary school children. The sequences were recorded in two different schools: one, which I shall refer to as the 'pendulum' sequence, was recorded in the East Midlands; the other, the 'mining' sequence, was recorded in the north-east of England. In the 'pendulum' sequence there were six children (three girls and three boys) aged between 10 and 11 years, and a female teacher. The children were reporting back on experiments they had carried out with pendulums, and discussing their findings. The 'mining' sequence involved eight children (four girls and four boys) aged from 9 to 10 and a female teacher. These children were having a follow-up discussion after having seen a television programme on coal-mining (the school was situated in a mining area). In both cases the discussion was 'set up' to the extent that it was being recorded for research purposes. However, the work the children were engaged in was part of their normal classwork at the time.

Because the sequences were video-recorded we could observe teachers' and pupils' nonverbal behaviour as well as their talk (I shall return to this point below). We could also note any activities, etc. that accompanied the talk and that might contribute to the overall interpretation of what was going on. For instance, in the 'pendulum' sequence the seating arrangements were such that the teacher could more easily face the boys. In the 'mining' sequence the teacher was standing but turned more often towards the boys. In the 'pendulum' sequence a girl was helped by the teacher to adjust a slide on an overhead projector. Boys were not helped, but a boy was asked to focus the projector, and also to handle other equipment. In the 'mining' sequence the seating arrangements were such that the boys could more easily see a model pit that was used for part of the lesson. A boy was also asked to put on some miner's equipment. On any one occasion such factors may, of course, be coincidental, but it is interesting that they were similar to aspects of classroom organisation recorded in the other general studies mentioned above (p. 128).

Having transcribed each video-recorded sequence we made various measures of the amount of talk contributed by each pupil. The number of turns and the number of words for each pupil are given in Table 9.1.

On average, boys contributed more in each sequence, both in terms of the number of turns taken and the number of words uttered. There were, however, intra-group differences: there were quieter boys and more talkative girls – including one particularly talkative girl in the 'mining' sequence. Clearly we could not make any generalizations on the basis of word- and turn-counts from such small samples: as with the aspects of classroom activities and organization mentioned above our results at this point simply confirmed that the distribution of talk in our groups was similar to that recorded in work carried out in other classrooms and with larger samples of pupils (such as French & French 1984, and Sadker & Sadker 1985).

When we came to examine more closely the interactional mechanisms by which boys obtained more turns than girls, we found differences between the two sequences. I shall describe briefly the findings from each sequence in turn.

TABLE 9.1 Contribution to classroom talk from girl and boy pupils in 'pendulum' and 'mining' sequences

Pupils	Amount spoken		
	Total words spoken	Total spoken turns	Average words per turn
'Pendulum' sequence			
Sarah	79	17	4.6
Laura	20	5	4.0
Donna	37	5	7.4
Unidentified girls	18	9	2.0
Total girls	154	36	4.3
Matthew	133	23	5.8
Trevor	83	20	4.1
Peter	55	10	5.5
Unidentified boys	48	20	2.5
Total boys	319	73	4.4
'Mining' sequence			
Kate	127	9	14.1
Lorraine	13	7	1.8
Anne	23	8	2.9
Emma	8	4	2.0
Unidentified girls	—	—	
Total girls	171	28	6.1
Mark	47	9	5.2
Ian	80	23	3.5
John	35	5	7.0
Darren	101	15	6.7
Unidentified boys	3	2	1.5
Total boys	266	54	4.9

The 'pendulum' sequence

This sequence was one in which pupils apparently had a great deal of freedom to contribute. However, there were differences between how girls and boys began an interchange with the teacher. When selecting pupils to speak by name the teacher chose girls rather more often than boys (11 occasions for girls and eight for boys). It was most common, however, for pupils simply to chip in to answer questions, without raising their hands or being selected by name. Boys were at a clear advantage here, chipping in or volunteering responses on 41 occasions, as opposed to girls' 13.

It seemed, then, as if boys were able to use the relatively unconstrained atmosphere to dominate the talk. However, certain aspects of the teacher's behaviour may also have favoured the boys. An example of this is the teacher's gaze behaviour, which we were able to analyse for part of the sequence. For the portion of the video-tape in which the teacher was clearly in view and in which we could measure her gaze towards the pupils, we found that she looked towards the boys for 60 per cent of the time and towards the girls for 40 per cent of the time. The following brief extract provides an illustration of the distribution of the teacher's gaze and shows how this may encourage the boys to participate more. The extract comes about half way into the sequence, when pupils have finished reporting on their experiments and are engaged with the teacher in a more general discussion of their results.

Questions are numbered in sequence.[3]

.... = teacher's gaze towards the girls
----------- = teacher's gaze towards the boys
> (Where gaze is not marked this is because the teacher is looking elsewhere – for instance, at the overhead projector.)

Teacher: If you have a pendulum (.) which we established last

week was a weight a mass (.) suspended from a string

or whatever (.) and watch I'm holding it with my hand

so it's at rest at the moment (.) what is it that makes

the pendulum swing in a downward direction for

instance till it gets to there? [1] ⎰(.) just watch it
Matthew: ⎱gravity

Teacher: What is it Matthew? [2]

Matthew: Gravity

Teacher: ⌈Yes (.)⌉now we mentioned gravity when we were
Boy: ⌊((xxx))⌋

Teacher: actually doing the experiments but we didn't discuss it

too much (.) OK so it's gravity then that pulls it

down (.) what causes it to go up again at the other

side? [3]

Boy: ⌈Force   the force⌉

Boy: ⌊The string   Miss⌋it gets up speed going down.

Teacher: It gets up speed going⌈down (.) does⌉anyone know the
Boy: ⌊(force)(xxx)⌋

Teacher: word for it when you get up speed? [4] (.) as in a car

when you press the pedal? [5]

Boy: ⌈accelerate⌉
Boy: ⌊momentum⌋

Teacher: You get momentum (.)⌈Matthew (.)⌉it accelerates
Matthew: ⌊(xxx)⌋

Teacher: going down doesn't it and it's the (.) energy the force that it builds up that takes it up the other side (.)

watch (.) and see if it's the same (.) right (.) OK (.)

em (.) anything else you notice about that? [6] (.) so

it's gravity what about the moon? [7] (.) that's a bit

tricky isn't it? [8] (.) is ⌈there grav⌉ ity on the

Boys: ⌊(xxx)   ⌋

Teacher: moon? = [9]

Boys: = No no it would float

Teacher: There isn't gravity on the moon? [10] (.)

Several: No

Matthew: There is a certain amount

Teacher: A certain amount Matthew? = [11]

Matthew: =⌈ (xxx) ⌉

Boy: ⌊ Seven ⌋ times less

Teacher: You reckon it's seven?[12]

Boy: Times less than on earth

Teacher: Yes (.) well it's a it's a difficult figure to arrive at but

it is between six and seven

The transcript shows, first of all, that the teacher is looking much more often towards the boys. The teacher is also more often looking towards the boys at critical points, when a question requires to be answered. (Of the 12 questions, eight are directed towards the boys and four towards the girls).

Of the four girls' questions, two (numbers 4 and 6) occur after a last-minute switch of gaze from the boys to the girls. Another (number 8), although we coded it as a question to give it the benefit of the doubt, seems to function more as an aside, or a comment on the activity, than as an attempt to elicit information.

Although in the 'pendulum' sequence, then, the boys seemed able to contribute more to the discussion by simply 'chipping in', our analysis of the teacher's gaze behaviour during a portion of the interaction suggests she may be distributing her attention selectively between the pupils and thus favouring the boys. It is also worth noting from the transcript that boys' speech often overlaps the teacher's. General 'muttering' from the boys occurs at various points during the interaction and may have the function of attracting, or maintaining the teacher's attention.

The 'mining' sequence

The teacher in this sequence had a different teaching style. The interaction was lively but kept more directly under the teacher's control: pupils rarely called out an answer – normally they raised their hands and were selected to speak. The following interchange is an example of the commonest way pupils obtained a speaking turn. Gaze is marked as in the 'pendulum' transcript. The superscript shows the order of hand-raising.
Interchange between teacher and Kate:

		Notes
	--------------------------------	Teacher looking at boys but can see girls. As K's hand goes up, teacher turns to look at girls. By the time boys' hands are raised, teacher has already begun to turn to girls. By the time E's hand rises, teacher's gaze is already directed towards K.
Teacher:	How did they know that	
	(KJMEA)	
	-----------------------------	
	those men were alive? (.)	
	.....	
	yes	
	....	
Kate:	Miss they were knocking	
	....	
Teacher:	They were knocking	

(K = Kate; J = John; M = Mark; E = Emma; A = Anne)

Here the teacher looks towards the boys then switches to the girls. Kate is selected to answer, and hers was the first hand raised. The teacher seemed to have a strategy of occasionally selecting a quiet child whose hand was not raised and encouraging them to answer (Lorraine and Emma obtained all their speaking turns this way, and Anne half of hers). On the whole, though, when she was in a position to see it, the teacher responded to the first or most decisively raised hand (Kate, and the boys, obtained most of their speaking turns this way). The teacher was in fact extraordinarily sensitive to the first hand raised. Presumably she was responding intuitively to this (and no doubt to additional nonverbal cues) as hands were raised very rapidly and, in analysing the sequence, we had to play the video frame by frame to determine the order of hand-raising. Although the teacher appeared quite directive, therefore, this gave the pupils considerable scope: they could ensure they were selected to speak more often if they were confident enough to raise their hands first.

As with the 'pendulum' sequence there seemed to be an interaction here between the behaviour of different participants that guaranteed the boys (on average) more speaking turns:

First, more confident pupils (who tended more often to be boys) simply raised their hands first and more decisively, thereby attracting the teacher's attention.

Second, we were able to analyse the teacher's gaze behaviour for the whole of the 'mining' sequence. This analysis showed that, as with the 'pendulum' sequence, the teacher's gaze was more often directed towards the boys (for 65 per cent of the time as opposed to 35 per cent of the time towards the girls). This occurred during general exposition as well as during more interactive parts of the sequence. Furthermore, when the teacher began to formulate a question with her gaze towards the boys she tended to maintain this gaze direction (unless a girl's hand was raised before a boy's and attracted her attention). However, on those (fewer) occasions in which the teacher began a question with her gaze directed towards the girls she tended to switch towards the boys half-way through the question, or to switch back and forth between girls and boys. This overall pattern of gaze behaviour may give boys generally more positive feedback and encourage them to respond to questions when they came.

Third, all the girls (and not just Kate) did frequently raise their hands during this sequence. Even Emma, the quietest pupil, often had her hand in the air. As in the example given above, however, Emma normally raised her hand just after the teacher's gaze had been directed towards the pupil she intended to select to speak. Such girls' hand-raising strategies, then, contribute to their relatively poor level of participation just as much as many boys' strategies enable them to contribute more.

4. Male dominance reconsidered

Many points arising from a consideration of classroom talk, and from the exploratory analysis of teacher and small-group inter-action that I have just described, can illuminate some of the issues raised at the beginning of this chapter in relation to gender differences in conversation. For instance, points, (i), (ii) and (iii) (see section 2, p. 125–7) concerned difficulties in identifying certain formal features of talk; in attributing the use of one set of features to women and another to men (thus establishing a 'female style' and a 'male style'); and in attributing a particular function to formally identified features. The exploratory study (in common with other studies of classroom talk) raises problems for the notion of female and male styles, first because differences between girls and boys are not categorical: boys may take more turns on average, but there are quiet boys (and more talkative girls). Second, while those who dominate classroom talk (in this case largely by talking more often) do tend to be boys, different interactional mechanisms are used in each context. In the rela-tively informal atmosphere of the 'pendulum' discussion, boys chip in much more often than girls. In the 'mining' sequence talk seems to be more overtly under the teacher's control and pupils (of either sex) rarely chip in: boys are selected to talk more often by the teacher, but this seems to be related to their ability to raise their hands more decisively and fractionally earlier than girls. It appears then that certain 'interactional resources' are available that might allow a speaker to have more say in a discussion, but that the resources available differ in different contexts. Rather than there being a particular set of 'controlling tactics', would-be dominant speakers would need to select features as appropriate to a context (taking account of the roles played by participants, the activities in which they are engaged, etc.).

Under point (iv) (p. 127) I mentioned that a complete analysis of inequalities in talk would need to take account, not only of a range of linguistic factors, but also of nonverbal components of an interaction. It's worth pointing out here that many studies of talk have relied on audio-recordings and transcripts and so cannot take account of nonverbal features, nor (reliably) of any accompanying activities. Studies of gender and classroom life, or classroom interaction (carried out perhaps more often by sociologists or educationists than by linguists or conversation analysts) have often seen talk as playing a part *along with other factors* in establishing and maintaining inequalities between girls and boys. It might be useful now to have more detailed studies showing the interplay between these different factors. This would mean expanding the metaphorical box of 'interactional resources' to include nonverbal features that interact with talk and may fulfil similar functions. In the 'mining' sequence, for instance, hand-raising strategies were crucial in obtaining (or not obtaining) speaking rights. Gaze was an important interactional mechanism in both sequences (though we were not able to analyse its use by pupils). Other features such as posture and gesture no doubt played their part, though they did not form part of our analysis. Finally, other accompaniments to the talk such as seating arrangements and the positioning and use of equipment may have contributed to the overall achievement of 'male dominance', though more work is needed to see how, on any one occasion, such factors interact with talk. There is, of course, a methodological problem here, in that, while it would seem useful to have a more complete record of what is going on in any sequence of talk, two or three video cameras would be needed even to cope with a small group discussion (let alone a whole class). Any observation may affect what is going on but the introduction of so much hardware would probably be unacceptably intrusive. In our exploratory study we lost some (no doubt) valuable information in the interests of remaining rather less intrusive.

Finally, point (v) (see p. 127) mentioned certain problems in relation to the notion of male 'dominance' itself. The studies of classroom talk that I have discussed suggested that to speak of boys 'dominating' classroom talk, while a useful shorthand, may risk oversimplifying things. It seems more plausible to argue that there is an interaction between the behaviour of all participants: for instance, the greater attention paid by teachers towards boys may encourage boys' fuller participation, which in turn encourages greater attention from the teacher, and so on. It is likely that everyone is an accomplice in the tendency by boys to contribute more to classroom talk – girls too by, arguably, using the resources available in the interaction to contribute less.

The points made above have theoretical implications, and also practical implications for anyone wishing to analyse gender differences in talk. Studies of classroom talk are, however, also important in relation to (educational) policies on gender. For instance, if a whole variety of linguistic and nonlinguistic features can be used to achieve or support 'male dominance', how successful are local solutions (such as changes in teachers' classroom management strategies) likely to be?

Furthermore, if inequalities in talk between girls and boys are regarded as normal by all parties, they are likely to be resistant to change. If girls are encouraged to become more assertive, and to adopt conversational tactics more commonly associated with boys, will such behaviour be tolerated by others or regarded as deviant?

Notes

1. This article relies for part of its discussion on an analysis of classroom talk that I carried out with an Open University colleague, David Graddol.

    The 'Pendulum' extract comes from data originally collected by Derek Edwards, Neil Mercer and Janet Maybin for their ESRC-funded project 'The Development of Joint Understanding in the Classroom' (ESRC No. C00232236). I am very grateful to Derek, Neil and Janet, and to the East Midlands school where the 'Pendulum' extract was recorded, for allowing access to these data. The 'Mining' extract comes from material collected at Escomb school, County Durham. Again, I am grateful to the staff and pupils for allowing one of their lessons to be video-recorded. (In both cases, I have changed the children's names to protect their identity, and the teachers are not referred to by name.)

2. West and Zimmerman (1983) have revised their operational definition of an interruption, see pp. 113–14, note 4. This revised definition does not, however, affect the main argument here.

3. Questions are marked with a ?. Utterances so marked were assessed by us to be functioning as questions, sometimes because of their syntactic form, but at other times for other reasons; we relied on cues such as intonation, but our interpretation relied on intuition. It is in fact difficult, on any occasion, to itemise the cues that are being attended to and that lead to an utterance being interpreted as a question.

Chapter 10

Talking shop: sex and status as determinants of floor apportionment in a work setting

Nicola Woods

1. Power, status and floor apportionment

Recent research has shown that the power and status of conversational participants has a strong and predictable effect upon the way in which interaction is organised. The following study aimed to investigate this phenomenon by examining the influence of the two bases of occupational status and gender: in brief, to examine whether 'powerful' persons (i.e. those in high occupational positions and men) command a dominating role within conversation and thereby gain for themselves a disproportionate amount of floor space, or more simply 'speaking time'.

An important element of the method used here was that the variables of gender and occupational status were separated out for the purposes of the analysis. It has often been suggested (see, for example, O'Barr & Atkins 1980) that quantitative findings on male dominance in conversation can be explained to a significant extent by the fact that males on average hold higher-status positions than do women: that is, it is not simply gender which causes men to dominate and women to defer. If this is true it should also follow that: (a) where women are in positions of power they will dominate conversation in ways similar to men; and (b) that where men are in subordinate positions their dominant behaviour will diminish or disappear. By sampling interactions in a work setting which included both sexes in the roles of 'boss' and 'subordinate', the present study was able to put these assumptions to the test by examining the variables of gender and occupational status and their relative influence on patterns of floor apportionment.

1.1 The proposed model: a 'simplest systematics for turn-taking'

In order to study conversational behaviour and the relative effects of gender and occupational status, the model of turn taking proposed by Sacks, Schegloff and Jefferson (1974) was employed. This model accounts for the system of turn taking within 'ordinary' conversation. In the first instance, the researchers lay down certain 'facts' about the organisation of this type of interaction. For instance, they argue that conversation is carried out in such a way as to ensure that 'only one party speaks at a time', and that 'speaker change recurs' (1974: 10). Further, they suggest that conversation is fairly fluid – that is to say, gaps and overlaps occur only rarely. Having highlighted these basic 'facts' the researchers then proceed to make one fundamental assumption about the turn-taking system: they suggest that speaker change can only meaningfully occur at transition relevance places (TRPs). A TRP comes about when the current speaker reaches the end of a **unit-type** – that is, the meaningful end of what he or she is saying. At this point, and only at this point, it is relevant and 'meaningful' for another party to take and hold the floor. (Within this study 'holding' the floor means only *a turn at* holding the floor, and is equated simply with a speaking turn. I acknowledge Edelsky's argument that a party who is speaking may not in fact be in full 'possession' of the floor, and conversely that 'it is possible to have the floor when one is not talking' (1981: 406)). Working from this basic assumption – that there are particular places within conversation where speakership can change – the researchers go on to outline three basic rules that account for which participant taking part in a conversation does in fact take over as speaker.

The first and most powerful rule applies when 'current speaker selects next speaker'. This rule (rule 1) can come into operation in a number of ways: the current speaker can select the next speaker by name, or by asking a direct question – and thus providing one half of an adjacency pair which requires some answer – or alternatively by nonverbal cues such as pointing, nodding, etc. If rule 1 is put into action by the current speaker it is then inappropriate for anyone but the selected speaker to take the floor. If, however, the next speaker is not selected – if rule 1 does not come into operation – then at the TRP it is open to any party to 'self-select': that is, the 'right' to speak falls upon the participant who selects him or herself first – this is rule 2. The last rule – rule 3 – comes into operation when rules 1 and 2 break down. Only in this case, does the current speaker have the right to take up speakership once again.

This then, in brief, is the model of conversational turn taking proposed by Sacks, Schegloff and Jefferson. However, before moving on, one further point ought to be made about the system. At the risk of stating the axiomatic, it should be said that the whole system can only be seen to work – indeed can only work – if the participants within conversation are paying attention to one another. Schegloff (1972: 379) has suggested in fact that listeners or 'hearers' make known their attention by using 'assent terms': for instance, *mm*, *yeah*, *yes*, *right*, etc. Schegloff argues that these terms (also known as 'minimal responses' and 'back channel' speech) are not interruptions but rather 'demonstrations of continued, co-ordinated hearership' (1972: 380), and that they are thus an essential part of any meaningful conversation.

Later this model will be used as a basis from which a number of hypotheses will be generated in order to test whether powerful participants dominate conversational organisation and thereby gain for themselves a disproportionate amount of floor apportionment. However, before moving on to this, it would be as well to consider a number of other studies which have investigated the relationship between participants' power and dominance of conversational organisation.

1.2 The influence of the power base of gender on conversational organisation and floor apportionment

Possibly the best known study of gender and floor apportionment is that designed and executed by Zimmerman and West (1975). These researchers investigated the influence of gender upon the turn-taking system by examining both occurrences of 'simultaneous speech' (defined by overlap and interruption) and 'silences'. From recordings of 31 two-party interactions the researchers found, with reference to simultaneous speech, that while the distribution of overlaps and interruptions was symmetrical within same-sex interaction, within mixed-sex conversations a rather different pattern emerged: 'virtually all the interruptions and overlaps were by the male speakers (98 per cent and 100 per cent, respectively)' (1975: 115). Further to this, Zimmerman and West suggested that such patterns of interruption and overlap, together with a male tendency to delay their use of assent terms to female parties, actually accounted for the disproportionate amount of female silence within male-female interaction, which did not occur in same-sex conversation. From the basis of these findings the researchers concluded that through such 'violations' of the turn-taking model 'men deny equal status to women as conversational partners with respect to rights to the full utiliz- ation of their turns and support for the development of topics' (1975: 125).

The study carried out by Zimmerman and West has provided the strongest evidence to suggest that the power generally assumed by males is reflected in domination of conversational interaction. Other studies which have supported these findings include that carried out by Esposito (1979), who found in a study of children's speech that 'boys at 3.5 to 4.8 years have been shown to interrupt girls in a way similar to the way that men have been shown to interrupt women' (1979: 218). Also Edelsky (1981) discovered that when the floor could be distinguished as an 'Fl' type – that is, a floor which is characterised by 'mono- logues' and 'single-party talk' – then men seemed to dominate by taking turns which were '$1\frac{1}{4}$ to nearly 4 times longer than women's' (Edelsky 1981: 415). Finally, Hirschman (1973, 1974) suggested from the study of a number of mixed and same-sex dyadic conversations, that the most 'striking' difference between male and female organisation of conversation is to be found within their differing use of assent terms: in particular, that 'females use the mm, hmm response much more often than males' (1974: 249).

It is clear, therefore, that there is much evidence to suggest that firstly, a significant difference exists in the way that men and women organise conversation; and secondly, that the power assumed by males is reflected in their domination of mixed-sex interaction and thus also in disproportionate floor-holding. However, to present only the above studies would be to give a somewhat biassed view of the effects that the power base of gender has been found to have upon conversational organisation, since there are other studies which have provided conflicting evidence. Some of this research also highlights the effects that occupational status (and other forms of 'expertise') have upon floor apportionment.

1.3 The influence of the power bases of expertise and occupational status on floor apportionment

Leet-Pellegrini's (1980) study of the power bases of gender and expertise suggested that while women generally tended to use more assent terms than men (a result which supports Hirschman's findings), nevertheless male dominance was not a salient feature of mixed-sex conversation. In fact, Leet-Pellegrini's study showed that such domination only occurred when the power base of expertise was added to that of gender: that is, when males were given specific information that allowed them to be 'experts' within a conversational encounter. Thus Leet-Pellegrini's discovery that 'The emergence of power . . . was not based primarily upon expertise *per se*, nor upon gender *qua* gender, but upon a subtle interplay between the two' (1980: 103) suggests that the power inherent in being male is not enough in itself to establish dominance within mixed-sex conversation.

The research of Beattie (1981) has also cast some doubt upon the validity of the 'male domination' theory of conversational organisation: within his study of interruption patterns in mixed-sex university tutorials he found that 'Sex differences had no significant effect on the amount or type of interruption' (1981: 31–2). However, while no significant difference between the sexes was found, Beattie's results did show that occupational status had a fairly dramatic effect upon interruption patterns: namely, that 'In terms of overall frequency of interruption, the high-status individuals in these groups – tutors in university tutorials – were interrupted significantly more frequently than they themselves interrupted' (1981: 15).

These patterns of interruption are somewhat surprising since, as Beattie himself points out, interruptions are invariably seen as a 'reflection of dominance in social interaction' (1981: 32), and thus it would have been expected that tutors as the dominant members of the tutorial groups would have used interruption more frequently than students. However, these results may be explained by taking into account the fact that a tutor's role within tutorial discussion is to 'encourage students to talk' (1981: 32); and, therefore, that this particular occupational aim of tutors distorts the more usual findings which reflect a positive correlation between speaker status and frequency in the use of interruption.

Previous research designed to investigate the influence that the power bases of gender and expertise or occupational status have upon conversational organisation and floor apportionment can thus be seen to have brought forth a number of conflicting results. So, while certain hypotheses based upon Sacks, Schegloff and Jefferson's turn-taking system will now be put forward in order to test the conjecture that 'powerful' persons will dominate conversation, nevertheless it should be noted that the somewhat contradictory nature of previous research dictates that these hypotheses be in all senses open to question, and thus falsification. Bearing this in mind, the following hypotheses can now be made about the conversational behaviour of 'powerful' participants; that is, (a) men, and (b) women of high occupational status.

1.4 The Proposed Hypotheses:

1. *Powerful participants will be selected to speak more often than nonpowerful participants (rule 1).* This is hypothesised since the results of Hirschman, Edelsky and an initial pilot study carried out to test the feasibility of this present research suggested that powerful parties dominate conversation not only 'because of their own efforts, but also because of the support that they receive from others'.

2. *Powerful participants will self-select more often than nonpowerful participants (rule 2).* The testing of a similar hypothesis by Esposito (1979) showed no such effect.

3. *Powerful participants will interrupt and overlap others more frequently than nonpowerful participants.*[1] Support for this hypothesis has been provided by the research of Esposito (1979) and Zimmerman and West (1975), but questioned by Beattie in 1981.

4. *Powerful participants will be interrupted and overlapped less frequently than nonpowerful participants.* (As above).

5. *Powerful participants will speak through more Transition Relevance Places than nonpowerful participants (i.e. will continue speaking without a pause between unit-types).* A similar hypothesis was supported by Edelsky (1981) in her investigation of floors of an 'Fl' type.

6. *Powerful participants will take up speakership after a pause more often than nonpowerful participants. (Rule 3).* To my knowledge this hypothesis has never been tested.

7. *Powerful participants will use assent terms less frequently than nonpowerful participants.* The term 'assent' is here defined, following Schegloff (1972:380), as a 'demonstration of continued, co-ordinated hearership'. Thus, *mm, yeah, yes, right* and other back-channel responses will be considered as forms as assent. Such terms will *not* be classified as self-selections, overlaps or interruptions unless they are used in such a way as to allow either an initiation of, or intrusion into, speech.

    Support for this hypothesis has come from the research of both Leet-Pellegrini (1980) and Hirschman (1973, 1974).

8. *Powerful participants will receive more terms of assent than nonpowerful participants.* (See above).

2. Methodology

In all, nine recordings of triadic conversations were made of interaction between work colleagues of differing occupational status. Six of these were designed to test the hypotheses: three involved one female of high occupational status with one male and one female subordinate; and the remaining three involved one male of high occupational status with one female and one male subordinate. Within the three conversations where females held 'boss' positions the male subordinates were second in the occupational hierarchy, and the female subordinates third. Within male 'boss' interaction the female subordinates were the same subjects who had themselves been recorded as 'boss' in the conversational structure outlined above. Within these conversations the females held second position in the occupational hierarchy, and male subordinates were third. (Fig. 10.1 shows, in a graphic form, the different conversational structures). Such a sample of recorded interaction allowed not only an examination of the conversational behaviour of separate interacting individuals in mixed-sex, different occupational status conversation, but also allowed comparisons to be drawn from the examination of the same subjects' behaviour in both 'boss' and subordinate occupational positions.

In order to account for any extraneous variables occurring because of the differing personalities of the subjects, three 'control' conversations were recorded between: (a) the three females who had been recorded in both 'boss' and subordinate positions; (b) the three males who had been recorded in 'boss' positions; (c) three males, one of whom had been used twice as a male subordinate within conversations where females held 'boss' positions. (This latter situation was necessitated by the fact that very few males held occupational positions lower than females.) These recordings of same-sex conversations provided a control against which the effects of the power base of gender could be measured. Control of occupational status was rather more difficult to achieve since most subjects were, of course, at different levels in the occupational hierarchy. However, the above same-sex control conversations were also between near-equal occupational status participants, and thus these recorded interactions provided, to a large extent, a control against which the effects of the power base of occupational status could be measured.

All recordings were made surreptitiously by concealing a tape recorder within a recording studio-cum-office at the subjects' place of work. (This context was chosen since, even if the tape

Conversation No.1

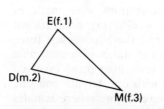

Conversation No.2

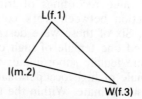

Conversation No.3

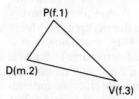

Conversation No.4

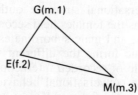

Conversation No.5

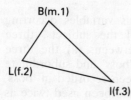

Conversation No.6

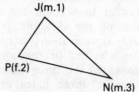

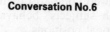

E,D,H,L etc. = Subject's initials
m,f = Male, female
1,2,3 = Position in occupational hierarchy

FIG. 10.1 Triadic conversations between work colleagues of differing occupational status

recorder had been discovered, the subjects would have been less likely to think its presence unusual – in fact no such 'discovery' was made.) The informants were told of the recordings only after the event, at which stage they were given the option to refuse permission for the tapes to be used: no such refusals actually occurred.

The recordings made were of varying lengths: between 14 and 32 minutes. From each recording a passage of two minutes was randomly selected, using random number selection function on a standard calculator and fast-forwarding the tape counter to the number randomly selected. If it was found that the preceding two-minute slot contained basically either one-party floor hold-ership, or lengthy sustained silences then the passage was rejected and another two-minute slot was randomly selected: in fact only one passage was rejected in this way. Results were obtained by simply calculating the frequency with which subjects used self-selection, interruption, assent, etc.

3. Results

3.1 General trends

Results showed that when the two power bases of gender and occupational status are at work, then the former – gender – tends to exert the greater influence on floor apportionment. Essentially, while the power base of occupational status did influence the way that both men and women organised conversation (generally, speakers in high occupational positions spent more time holding the floor than their subordinates, and more specifically in two cases the same speakers gained more floor space in 'boss' rather than subordinate positions), nevertheless even when women held high-status occupational positions male subordinates still organised the interaction in a way that allowed them to dominate the floor: for instance, by interrupting more often, speaking through more TRPs and giving less assent to women participants.

A basic assumption that underpins the results put forward is, of course, that it was the independent variables of gender and occupational status that influenced floor apportionment rather than any extraneous variables that occurred merely because of the differing personalities of the subjects. Results of the control conversations recorded to test the validity of this assumption tended to confirm that this was indeed the case: in brief, no evidence emerged to suggest that the results were in any way confounded.

3.2 Detailed findings for the eight hypotheses

3.2.1 *Powerful participants will be selected to speak more often than nonpowerful participants*

Occupational status did not affect selection, and thus with regard to this power-base, hypothesis 1 could not be supported:

firstly, Table 10.1 shows that those in 'boss' positions are never selected by others; and secondly, it can be seen that women are selected more often in subordinate than in high occupational status positions – 3 and 0 respectively. However, it is interesting to note that the collapsed results of the male subordinates in (A) show that they are selected no less than 12 times, although this apparent influence of gender-based power is not reflected in (B). It would thus be an interesting area of further study to investigate whether male selection is a salient feature of mixed-sex conversation where only one male is present with two or more females, or more generally, simply where female participants outnumber male participants.

TABLE 10.1

	A			B		
Occ. status	1	2	3	1	2	3
Sex	E	M	F	M	F	M
Selection	0	12	1	0	3	1

(Tables 10.1–10.9 show the integrated results of the six 'experimental' conversations: 'A' shows the collapsed results of the three conversations in which female parties held 'boss' positions, while 'B' gives the collapsed results of interactions in which male parties had the highest occupational status.)

3.2.2 Powerful participants will self-select more often than nonpowerful participants

This hypothesis could not be supported, since neither of the two power bases had any significant or regular effect upon self-selection, and thus these results are in line with those put forward by Esposito (1979).

TABLE 10.2

	A			B		
Occ. status	1	2	3	1	2	3
Sex	F	M	F	M	F	M
Self selection	18	15	21	17	16	18

3.2.3 Powerful participants will be more likely to interrupt and overlap others

The results to emerge from the testing of this hypothesis are rather complicated. Firstly, it could be argued that occupational status does influence frequency of interruption since as Table 10.3 shows, the same females use six successful interruptions in 'boss' positions compared to only one when they are subordi-nates. However, in (A) it is shown that the influence of gender overrides that of occupational status: male subordinates using successful interruption nine times. Further, it should also be noted that in (B) there is no difference in frequency between the male bosses' and male subordinates' use of successful interruptions, but that nevertheless both outweigh the use of this type of intrusion by female parties.

Patterns of unsuccessful interruption also illuminate the over-riding power of gender: Table 10.3 shows that women's inter-ruptions fail far more often than men's. Indeed, taken as a whole, it can be seen that out of 21 interruptions women actually gain the floor on only 11 occasions; while men, on the other hand, gain the floor by the use of this type of intrusion in 17 out of a possible 20 instances. These results would support the find-ings of Esposito (1979) and Zimmerman and West (1975), but stand, to some degree at least, in contradiction to those put forward by Beattie (1981).

Finally, the only result to emerge from this study with refer-ence to overlap is the surprising infrequency with which they were used. However, this can probably be accounted for by the rather strict criterion used to define this term.

TABLE 10.3

Occ. status	1	2	3		1	2	3
		A				B	
Sex	F	M	F		M	F	M
Successful interruption	6	9	4		4	1	4
Unsuccessful interruption	3	1	3		0	4	2
Successful overlap	2	0	0		0	2	2
Unsuccessful overlap	0	0	0		0	0	0

3.2.4 Powerful participants will be less likely to be interrupted and overlapped

Table 10.4 shows that this hypothesis, at least with reference to patterns of interruption, can be supported: firstly, with regard to the power base of occupational status, it is shown that both males and females in 'boss' positions are successfully interrupted less frequently than their subordinates; and secondly, the above highlights that the same women are successfully interrupted more often in subordinate than in high occupational positions – seven and two times respectively.

With reference to gender, (B) shows that males in the lowest occupational position are successfully interrupted less frequently

than their female superiors; and, maybe most telling, the subordinate females in (A) are interrupted no less than 11 times,
almost four times as often as their male counterparts in (B).

TABLE 10.4

	A			B		
Occ. status	1	2	3	1	2	3
Sex	F	M	F	M	F	M
Interrupted successfully	2	6	11	1	7	3
Interrupted unsuccessfully	1	4	1	5	1	0
Overlapped successfully	0	2	1	0	0	2
Overlapped unsuccessfully	0	0	0	0	0	0

*3.2.5 Powerful participants will speak through more Transition
Relevance Places than nonpowerful participants (i.e. will
continue speaking through a number of unit-types without a
pause)*

The result in Table 10.5 is possibly the most striking to have
emerged from this study. The testing of this hypothesis showed
that males speak through far more TRPs than females, and thus
hold significantly longer turns. This result is highlighted in both
(A) and (B): in (A) it can be seen that males hold turns that are
three times as long as their female 'bosses'; and similarly, in (B)
males in third position in the occupational hierarchy take turns
that are $2\frac{3}{4}$ times as long as the females who are occupationally
superior to them. Thus, while the power base of occupational
status can be seen at work (for instance, the same females speak
through more TRPs when they are in 'boss' rather than subordinate positions – 18 and 8 respectively; and in (B) male
'bosses' can be seen to speak through twice as many TRPs as
males beneath them in the occupational hierarchy), nevertheless,
gender can be seen to exert by far the greater influence over this
result.

Finally, it is interesting to view these results in the light of the
research carried out by Edelsky (1981). In the introduction it was
pointed out that Edelsky had found this type of result (i.e., that
males hold significantly longer turns than females) only within
floors that could be described as an 'Fl' type – that is, floors characterised by 'monologues' and 'single-party talk'. However, it will
be noted that this research actually rejected passages of conversation which contained only this type of floor holdership. The
results of this study would thus suggest that lengthy and sustained

male turns are not solely confined to floors in which 'turn-takers stand out from non-turn-takers' (1981:416), but also characterise other more 'co-operative' F2-type interaction. This result stands, therefore, to some degree at least, in contradiction to the findings put forward by Edelsky.

TABLE 10.5

Occ. status	A			B		
	I	2	3	I	2	3
Sex	F	M	F	M	F	M
Speak through T.R.P.	18	57	19	46	8	22

3.2.6 Powerful participants will continue speaking more frequently after a pause than non-powerful participants

While the small scale of these results means that they are not particularly striking, nevertheless Table 10.6 shows that males tend to speak after a pause more frequently than females; further, (B) shows that males in high occupational positions speak after $2\frac{1}{2}$ times as many pauses as do their male subordinates. Thus, both power bases can be seen to have had some influence over this result.

TABLE 10.6

Occ. status	A			B		
	I	2	3	I	2	3
Sex	F	M	F	M	F	M
Continue after pause	I	4	0	5	I	2

3.2.7 Powerful participants will use assent-terms less frequently than nonpowerful participants

Table 10.7 shows that females do not use assent terms any more frequently in subordinate than in 'boss' positions. Also (A) shows that there is very little difference in the use of assent of 'boss' females and the females beneath them in the occupational hierarchy. However, it is noticeable that in (B) male subordinates do use assent far more frequently than their higher-status colleagues. Finally, (A) shows that male subordinates use far fewer terms of assent than their female colleagues. Thus, while both power bases can be seen at work with regard to this hypothesis, nevertheless results show no regular pattern and therefore no clear trends can be pinpointed.

TABLE 10.7

		A			B		
		A			B		
Occ. status		1	2	3	1	2	3
Sex		F	M	F	M	F	M
Assent given		13	4	14	13	13	20

3.2.8 Powerful participants will receive more assent terms than nonpowerful participants

Here once again the strength of the gender power base can be seen to dominate: Table 10.8 (A) shows that male subordinates receive over $3\frac{1}{2}$ times more assent than their female 'bosses'; and, of course, most telling is the result that female 'bosses' in (A) receive only half as much assent as do the males in third subordinate position in (B). The influence of the occupational power base can be seen at work in a comparison of the two groups of males in (B), but this is not supported by a comparison of the same females in 'boss' and subordinate positions.

TABLE 10.8

		A			B		
Occ. status		1	2	3	1	2	3
Sex		F	M	F	M	F	M
Assent received		6	22	3	23	11	12

3.2.9 Effects on overall floor apportionment

At the outset of this research it was conjectured that powerful persons would spend a disproportionate amount of time holding the floor in mixed-sex differing occupational status conversations. The validity of this conjecture is highlighted in table 10.9 which shows – in seconds – the collapsed results of floor apportionment of the six individual conversations.

With reference to occupational status, (B) shows that men in 'boss' positions spend more time holding the floor than their subordinates; and also, a comparison of (A) and (B) shows that the same women hold the floor for 24 seconds longer in high rather than low occupational positions. The stronger and overriding effect of gender can be seen most significantly in (A) where it is shown that male subordinates hold the floor for almost half of the total conversation time, speaking over the total three two-minute conversations for 56 seconds longer than their female 'bosses'.

TABLE 10.9

	A			B		
Occ. status	1	2	3	1	2	3
Sex	F	M	F	M	F	M
Floor holding	117	173	70	168	93	99

The patterns of asymmetrical floor apportionment that have emerged in this study as a result of the influence of both power bases can be seen to be a result of all but one of the hypotheses (hypothesis 2). However, the strength of the influence of the power base of gender seems to have emerged from the results of three hypotheses in particular: hypotheses 3, 5 and 8. The testing of hypothesis 3 showed that males tend to succeed in gaining the floor by the use of interruption far more often than female participants: 85 per cent of men's interruptions were successful compared to only 44 per cent of women's. The following example, taken from conversation 3, gives an example of this dominating tactic used by men, where it is shown how a low occupational status male – speaker 'D' – interrupts his female superior. (Transcription notation is given in the Appendix, p. 174).

P (f):   . . .it would have been a bit too
D (m):   he speaks Bristolean   yeah . . .
V (f):   Bristolean?

In a similar way, the testing of hypothesis 5 further highlighted how men command a disproportionate amount of speaking time in male-female interaction: that is, by continuing to speak through significantly more transition relevance places than their female colleagues. The example below, taken from conversation 1, gives just one example of many instances in which this conversational tactic was used by male parties.

D (m):   The way he starts the meeting is he comes in and he
         blathers for about two minutes in Irish, err Scots
         Gaelic, and then turns round and says to them 'do you
         repeat?' = err and then asks 'what is that?',
H (f):   =mm

D: err, and then somebody will say 'Irish' and he'll say 'oh
         very clever' and then go on from that = so you
H: =mm

D: won't have missed much =
H: = no
E(f):   Does somebody always say Irish?
D: Err, no Gaelic you usually get and . . .

Finally, the results which emerged from testing hypothesis 8 showed that male domination of mixed-sex interaction is a consequence of not only the conversational behaviour of men themselves, but also of the support – in the form of assent – that they receive from female participants. This use of assent is illustrated in the examples given above. The first shows that while male speaker D dictates the flow of the interaction by his use of interruption, he is supported in this intrusion by female informant V who uses the assenting form 'Bristolean?'. Similarly, the second example shows how female participants not only let male speaker D continue through seven transition relevance places, but also provide him with assent at the very places (TRPs) where they could themselves take up speakership. Finally, also in this extract, it is worth noting that when female speaker E does manage to gain the floor, she only uses this space to ask a question of D and thus, by selecting him in this way, relinquishes the floor very quickly to the male conversational participant.

4. Summary and concluding remarks

The study was designed to investigate the effects of power and status on floor apportionment. It was conjectured that powerful persons – that is (a) men, and (b) women of high occupational status – would spend disproportionately more time holding the floor than nonpowerful persons. The validity of this conjecture was tested by generating a number of hypotheses from the basis of the model of conversational turn-taking proposed by Sacks, Schegloff and Jefferson. Results showed that, while the power base of occupational status did affect floor holding, nevertheless, gender exerted by far the stronger influence. It is therefore possible to conclude that when the two conflicting power bases of gender and occupational status are at work, then the former – gender – will have the stronger and overriding effect upon floor apportionment.

Having outlined this main result it should be noted in conclusion that the small-scale nature of this research means, of course, that further investigation is necessary if the general pattern of asymmetry – in the form of male domination – found within this study, is to be considered representative of male-female interaction generally. Perhaps the most useful line of enquiry for future research would be to examine a feature of male domination of conversation which has only been mentioned by this present study: namely, that the overriding influence of gender is a product of not only the conversational behaviour of males themselves, but also of the supporting role played by females. Future research might most usefully extend our knowledge, therefore, by differentiating between the influence on floor apportionment of the dominating tactics of men and the support given by women. (This could be achieved by employing an experimental approach in which women are instructed to withhold their use of supporting conversational features.) *In fine*, it is perhaps only by introducing such differentiations, and thereby establishing a more delicate framework for analysis, that the complexities of conversational organisation can be disentangled, and a greater, more intricate understanding of the effects of power and status upon such interaction be achieved.

Note

1. Following Zimmerman and West (1975), **interruption** is defined as an intrusion into speech which 'penetrates the boundaries of a unit-type prior to the last lexical constituent'; while **overlap** is defined as an intrusion where a 'speaker begins to speak . . . very close to a possible TRP' – that is, *not* before the 'last lexical constituent that could define a possible boundary of a unit-type' (1975:14).

Chapter 11

The wedding songs of British Gujarati women[1]

Viv Edwards and Savita Katbamna

1. Introduction

Recent Indian, Pakistani and Bangladeshi immigrants to Britain from both the Indian subcontinent and East Africa have access to a rich and varied oral culture which includes epic poetry, narrative and ritual insult. The present paper focusses on one particular aspect of this oral culture and one particular group: namely, the songs sung by women at weddings in the British Hindu Gujarati community.

A study of wedding songs is of interest partly because it helps to illuminate the social significance of marriage and marriage rites within Gujarati society and to explain the role of women in this community. But a study of this kind is also of more general interest in that it helps to redress the predominantly male bias in the existing literature. It is commonplace for ethnographers and anthropologists, not to mention secondary commentators on the linguistic situation of women (cf. Keenan 1974; Ardener 1975, 1978; Labov 1972c), to report that women tend not to be the main participants in highly valued speech events. This paper describes an exclusively female speech event accorded considerable status by the entire community. As such, it represents an important counterexample to the general assumptions about the role of women within the ethnography of speaking. It also leads us to wonder whether existing descriptions of speech communities have sometimes been guilty of oversimplification.

We will identify three main genres of wedding song – songs of solidarity, songs of insult and songs of conciliation. The social function which each of these genres fulfils will be explored and an attempt made to relate them to similar speech events in other cultures. Attention will be paid to the ways in which these songs reflect the values and structures of Gurajati society in general and the adaptation of that society to life in Britain. The transmission of this aspect of oral culture will also be considered, as, too, will the role of 'good singers'.

2. Collecting the songs

The present project was undertaken by two friends of longstanding: a Gujarati woman and a British woman. The Gujarati woman has a deep love for her language and culture which she has successfully communicated to her British linguist friend over a period of many years. Together we wanted to bring the insights of anthropology and sociolinguistics to a phenomenon which has long fascinated us both.

Yet the collection of the songs was by no means a simple task. The study of Gujarati wedding songs is considerably more accessible to an 'inside' researcher than an outsider (cf. Milroy 1980), but being Gujarati is not the only desideratum for an exploration of this area. As we will see, 'good singers' with wide repertoires are the exception rather than the rule. Having no pretensions about being a 'good singer' herself, the role of the Gujarati researcher was therefore to collect and help interpret the songs rather than to act as an informant herself. This was a long and sometimes difficult process.

Ironically, the best place to collect wedding songs is not necessarily weddings. The often noisy conditions make it difficult to obtain good-quality recordings. Words are sometimes forgotten and one song runs into another. In addition, some weddings have markedly better and more singing than others and, without the knowledge that certain 'good singers' will be present, it is impossible to know before the event how much information can usefully be collected. The obvious alternative was to record in their own homes people who were known to have wide repertoires.

The principle of reciprocity within relationships is fundamental in any society, but assumes particular importance in fieldwork with South Asian communities, where approaches to fieldwork which characterise much Western sociolinguistics (cf. Labov 1966; Trudgill 1974a) risk being dismissed as offensive or gauche. The researcher cannot simply make a request for information without seeming rude and arousing suspicion. This is due in part to an incredulity that something taken for granted as an integral part of Gujarati social life and culture should be an object of academic study. It may also be based on a fear that the observer's interest is both patronising and voyeuristic. But equally important is the necessity within many cultures to first perform a favour, thereby creating an obligation, before asking a favour. Western researchers' timetables are often too inflexible to meet such requirements.

In order to collect data, the Gujarati researcher, in her 'insider' capacity, began by inviting good singers to eat with her family and helping them with any problems that were discussed during the time they spent together. The feelings of obligation which were created through this contact made it acceptable for her to ask a favour in return. The women who supplied the materials on which this article is based were, for the most part, Gujarati Hindu women who came to Britian in the 1960s and early 1970s from East Africa and who have now made their homes in Harrow and surrounding areas of north-west London. It should be mentioned, however, that wedding songs are not restricted to this group. They can be heard not only in other Gujarati communities but in many other communities who came originally from northern India.

3. Marriage and marriage rites

Any discussion of the social significance of wedding songs depends in turn on an understanding of the social significance of marriage within Gujarati and indeed, other, Indian societies. Such an understanding will also help illuminate why wedding songs are a female domain, and the central role of women in this part of the wedding celebrations.

The ideal family in traditional village India is the patrilineal extended family living in a joint household under the direction of a senior male. In this setting the relationship between a father and his sons is potentially difficult in as much as sons are dependent on him both for their marriage arrangements and the organisation of the joint property, and mothers often play an important mediating role. Daughters are perceived in rather different terms. Fathers have a religious obligation to provide for their daughters' marriage but need not necessarily consult them on the choice of partner. At the beginning of a marriage, the new bride comes under the supervision of her mother-in-law and the wife of the head of the household and is not secure in the marital household until she has borne a son.

Important changes took place in this system of family organization in an East African setting. Individuals and not large blocks of patrilineal relatives were involved in migration and, because of the need for help and support in establishing a trading community, both collateral and affinal links were exploited in a kinship system which was functionally non-unilinear rather than patrilineal. In addition, the legal system did not recognise Hindu or Moslem law and the Partnership and Limited Liability Company enactments provided no support for the notion of joint household and joint ownership (Tinker 1977). This weakening of traditional values resulted in the development of new ideas on marriage and the conduct of daughters-in-law which helped young wives to persuade their husbands to form individual households. In Britain, where migrants have been exposed to forces very similar to those in East Africa, the indications are that the gradual erosion of traditional values is firmly underway. Brah (1978), for instance, suggests that both continuity and change can be detected among South Asian teenagers in Southall but that change is more apparent at the level of professed belief than practice.

Marriage plays a central role in Gujarati social organisation. Gujarati communities remain essentially endogamous groupings in which 'love marriages' (which take place outside the traditionally prescribed boundaries) are very strongly discouraged. Marriage provides for the strengthening of existing ties and the forging of new links and, although important changes have taken place in traditional family relationships, many of which are defined by marriage or marriage expectations, considerable pressure is still brought to bear on individuals to conform to the group norm.

Marriages in village India traditionally last for a week; in East Africa they were reduced to three days. In Britain, however, the more dispersed nature of the Gujarati and other Asian communities and the constraints of the normal working week have reduced the main celebrations to one and a half days for those most closely involved and half a day for the majority of the guests. Weddings which take place in London, for instance, may draw on guests from as far as the Midlands and the West Riding. None of these guests will be involved in work on the land, as would be likely to be the case in India, and a much smaller proportion than in East Africa will be self-employed. Distances to be travelled and the difficulties in getting time off work have therefore made the seven- or three-day wedding a practical impossibility.

There would also seem to be a certain degree of self-consciousness in conducting wedding rituals in Britain. In East Africa, Asians live predominantly or exclusively in Asian communities, thus facilitating the transfer of traditional practices. In Britain, however, much of the pomp and ceremony in the form, for instance, of processions and bands, would simply draw attention very firmly to cultural difference and various British-born informants have expressed embarrassment at the thought of incorporating these aspects into weddings in this country. Both practical considerations and an awareness of British intolerance towards cultural diversity would thus seem to have played a part in the modification of wedding ceremonies.

There is considerable variation in British Gujarati weddings. Generally speaking, however, certain differences from Indian and East African patterns are consistently to be found. Some preliminary rites, such as the invitation ceremony in which the Brahmin will personally write invitations to the closest family members are likely to be attended by fewer people. Others have been greatly conflated in time. The betrothal ceremony, for instance, sometimes immediately precedes the marriage; and the *haldi* ceremony, in which the body of the bride or groom is rubbed with a turmeric mustard-seed oil mixture takes place either the evening before or the morning of the ceremony. In village India, both ceremonies would be performed on an auspicious date fixed by the Brahmin.

The ritual significance of these ceremonies is extremely important and, as Henry (1975) remarks, they constitute 'the most comprehensive occurrence of symbolic activity' in Indian life. Songs accompany each of these rituals, but will not form the focus for the present study. Because they are attended by relatively few people, the singing which takes place is a very poor reflection of what it would be in village India and, if no 'good singer' is present, may not take place at all. The same is not true, however, of the *sanjina geet* – the independent gatherings of the bride's and groom's parties on the evening before the wedding – nor of the actual wedding ceremony. Increasingly taped music is played at Gujarati weddings. Yet there remains a sufficiently large number of 'good singers', and such activity retains sufficiently high status within the various communities, for wedding songs sung at these ceremonies to be considered a living part of contemporary British Gujarati culture rather than a relic of village India.

4. The transmission of wedding songs and the role of 'chorus leaders'

Much of Western culture is steeped in literature. Far more importance is attached to the written than to the spoken word and greater prestige is reserved for the person of letters than for the raconteur or folk singer. It is frequently assumed that societies which depart from Western literary norms are peopled with high-calibre exponents of the oral tradition. Reality would seem to be a long way from this romanticisation. Such societies do contain great story-tellers and singers of songs whose repertoires, by any standards, are impressive. They occupy a very important position in these societies and are invariably highly respected and acclaimed. None the less, they are relatively few in number, sometimes undergoing a very rigorous and specialised training (cf. Finnegan 1970), and they remain the exception rather than the rule.

This can be illustrated by the transmission and distribution of wedding-song skills in Gujarati women. There is an ancient tradition of verbal duelling in song and rhyme which can be traced back to the Sanskrit court, and on which wedding songs draw heavily. Although in weddings these songs are considered to form very much a female domain, outside that setting they are known, passively at least, by the whole community. One Ismaili[2] informant told of the ride in a hired bus when passengers passed the long hours by singing wedding songs on the journey to Dar-es-Salaam where her brother's wedding was taking place. Another informant told of community events which were regularly punctuated by a 'tug-of-war' in song between two sides which was usually initiated by the older women but in which everyone took part.

In a wedding setting, the women in certain families have a reputation for being good singers. This skill is defined both in terms of their voices and the extent of their repertoires. An accomplished woman is likely to have daughters who follow in her footsteps. The majority of families, however, make no claims to such skill. Interestingly, weddings provide a useful outlet for female talents which would be seriously frowned upon in other settings:

> Any dancing or singing in public is normally shunned because you are showing yourself off – men might look on you not as a woman but as a sex object. But a wedding song you can sing and nobody would look down on you.

> It is a very praiseworthy thing to sing in weddings while to sing on the stage is not approved of.

Good singers fulfil the role of 'chorus leaders' in weddings and less confident women will deliberately place themselves near the leaders. Most often tunes are either traditional or taken from popular films, so the words are the most important prop provided by the leader. When a woman gains a reputation for herself as a good singer her talents are likely to be widely recognised in the community:

> If this particular chorus leader has been to one wedding and then goes to another one, some of the relations who go to the second wedding know she can sing. They acquire a reputation for their ability to sing.

None the less, customary modesty is maintained and no woman would openly volunteer herself for this role:

> A chorus leader would have to be asked to do it because it's considered polite by everybody to be shy. Everyone pretends 'No, no, no, I can't sing!' 'Oh yes, you can!' 'No, no, I can't!' 'Come on, you can, we know you can. Come on, you sing. We'll back you up.' That's how they usually start.

Sometimes weddings are the scene for power struggles between two good singers:

> If there are two chorus leaders in a wedding they'll probably try and outdo each other. Sometimes one chorus leader starts and the other one also starts, but the one who's got the louder voice carries on and the other one joins in. Then she'll probably lead the next one.

Nor are the social implications of choosing a leader (both in terms of the prestige attached to this position and in the manipulation of relationship to one's own advantage) to be underestimated:

> Sometimes women are represented to further your interest. Someone might suggest a woman from your family as being very good at singing because they want to appear nice in your family for some reason. Maybe they've got a daughter to marry . . . there's a lot of politics that goes on.

Thus only some women present themselves or are represented as good singers. In so doing they fulfil a valued social role and gain considerable prestige. Prestige, however, does not exist in a vacuum. It is sometimes the end-product of subtle – and not so subtle – power struggles involving manipulation and guile on the part of the singer, her family and other members of the community.

5. The wedding songs

Three different kinds of song will be exemplified and analysed: songs of solidarity, songs of insult and songs of conciliation. They correspond broadly to the three stages – separation, transition and incorporation – which are normally held to characterise rites of passage, or ceremonies which ease the transition from one state to the next, of which marriage is clearly an example (cf. Van Gennep 1960).

5.1 Songs of solidarity

Songs of solidarity are associated with the *sanjina geet* ceremonies on the evening before the wedding. The assembly of relatively large numbers of the close family and guests marks the beginning of the wedding proper. In fact, this is the first of the ceremonies to which the majority of the guests will have been invited. The main function of the songs sung at this ceremony is to emphasise the family identity – to draw in the various members, particularly those related by marriage, to heal any rifts in family relations and to present a united front, as the bride's *jan* or the groom's *jan*, ready for the actual wedding ceremony the following day.

> It's trying to get the family together, making the grandfather, the
> uncle, all feel part of the family, making them closer through
> singing. If I was, say, the aunt and my husband's name appeared
> in the song I would feel I had a stake in this wedding. I'm not to
> be on the periphery.

The tensions between bride's and groom's *jans* will be discussed below. It is important that these tensions are not further compounded by any conflict within one party or the other.

> Really it's establishing the lineage . . . that the bride is the niece of
> so and so, the grand-daughter of so and so . . . The in-laws are the
> contentious party. You get them on your side and so you don't
> have two lots of in-laws against you.

Many of the tensions generated by the preparations for the wedding find their expression in songs which make fun of both parties. Such songs therefore function as a kind of steam valve, in the same way as for the *fatana* discussed below. A typical *sanjina geet* song for the groom's *jan*, is the following. The singers insinuate that the bride's family are not well off because they do not even possess a bullock cart, a very basic form of transport.

> Place some roses in a vase,
> Sprinkle *kum kum* and print the invitations.
> Send them to all four corners of the world,
> Send the first invitation to Rajkot:
>
> 'Lakshmiben, come early to our festivities,
> Bringing all the young and old of your household with you.'

But Amarsi, son-in-law, is in want of a bullock cart
And here we are getting ready for Vinodbhar's wedding.

By mentioning members of the other *jan* by name and poking
fun at them, the bridegroom's *jan* is helping to emphasise its own
sense of identity. The festive nature of the occasion, however,
gives rise not only to more serious songs of solidarity and songs
which mock the other *jan*, but to a gentle humour which allows
each *jan* to make fun of itself.

My wedding canopy is so beautiful, like the flowers in a lake.
Everyone comes to visit it, but stingy grandfather/maternal
uncle/paternal uncle/brother, etc. never comes.
Grandfather, etc. is stingy when such occasions arise.
The occasion will be gone tomorrow but the world's taunts will
remain.

5.2 Songs of insult (*fatana*)

Songs of insult, or *fatana*, are particularly interesting in terms of
social comment and the function which they serve. They take
place during the actual ceremony up to the critical point where
bride and groom walk around the fire and are considered man
and wife. Songs of insult are associated with weddings in other
cultures, too, though documentation tends to be fairly sparse
(see, e.g. H. Upadhyaya 1970; S. Upadhyaya 1973; Henry 1975;
Johnston 1975; Blake 1979). The fullest of these accounts, Henry
(1975) talks of the *gali* of eastern Uttar Pradesh, which differ
from *fatana* only in their obscenity. *Gali* commonly rely on insults
which impute immoral sexual behaviour – adultery, incest,
sodomy and pederasty. *Fatana*, however, concentrate on other
aspects of social behaviour and, although extremely abusive, fall
short of the obscene.

The tensions which surround a wedding are intense. The social
pressure on a girl to get married and on families to find suitable
partners for their children is considerable. Weddings provide
opportunities for displaying wealth and forging new links which
enable a family to consolidate or improve their position in the
social hierarchy. However, such opportunities bring not only
prestige but great worry and anxiety. Either party could withdraw
up until the last minute. Guests may be invited to the wedding,
but until the day arrives there is no way of knowing whether they
will think the occasion sufficiently important or well managed to
merit their attendance. If key figures are missing, or relatively
few guests arrive, the effect on the social standing of all
concerned could be disastrous. The bride, in particular, has very

ambivalent feelings about her transition from a family in which she has been loved and cherished to one where her status will be low and where she may meet varying degrees of hostility.

Fatana are clearly a manifestation of joking behaviour (cf. Radcliffe-Brown 1952). Such behaviour is found in relations where strong disjunctive and conjunctive forces are at work. This is certainly the case in Indian weddings. On the one hand it is very much in the interest of both sides to successfully bring about the marriage, thereby fulfilling religious obligations to their children and enhancing their own social standing; on the other hand, there are many potential conflicts inherent in this process: expectations of the various parties are extremely high and any failure to fulfil expectations is likely to be interpreted as a slight. The teasing and taunting of *fatana* offsets the hostility felt by either side and thus plays a very important role as a release valve for the tensions generated during both the preparations and the ceremonies. More than any of the other kinds of song, they clearly lay out the values and expectations of Gujarati society. They also provide real entertainment, and this is a role which should not be minimised.

It is extremely important, however, that the insults contained in *fatana* are ritual and not real. Any song which includes a blatant element of truth in relation to the other party is likely to cause great offence. Songs, for instance, which criticise the harsh treatment of the new bride by the senior daughter-in-law are likely to be avoided in the wedding of a second son. And where feeling is sufficiently strong over some aspect of the other side's behaviour, such as the standard of catering, for discretion to be temporarily overlooked, the party on the receiving end of the insult is likely to react very strongly.

5.3 Songs of conciliation (*valave*)

When the climax of the wedding ceremony is reached the mood of the singing changes from teasing and taunting to conciliation. The transition period is over and the time to recognise the couple's new married status has arrived. No longer do the women mock and ridicule the other side. Rather they entreat the bride to behave in a way which will bring honour on her family:

> You have got a *jeth*[3] like *Rama*[4], you have got a *jethani*[5] like *Sita*[6].
> You must respect them both, you with the flowers in your chinon.

These songs reassert the existing social order. Instead of mocking her husband's family, she is now told to consider them as her own and treat them with respect:

Think of your mother-in-law/husband's paternal uncle/husband's
maternal uncle/husband's brother etc. as your own mother/paternal
uncle/maternal uncle/brother, etc.

They appeal to the groom's side to treat her with kindness:

Oh new *vevai*[7] of a one and a quarter *lakh*[8]
Oh new *vevan*[9] of such a kind temperament
We are giving you our daughter
Please keep her as well as we kept her
If she asks for water give her milk
The bride is still only a child
Please look after her and take good care of her
Oh new *vevai* of a one and a quarter *lakh*
Oh new *vevan* of such a kind temperament.

The groom's family responds in the same spirit of reconcilia-
tion, acknowledging its responsibilities:

Oh *Jaisingh vevai* of one and a quarter *lakh*
Oh *Shushila vevan* of such a kind temperament
You have given us your daughter
We shall keep as well as you did
We shall not break our trust
When she asks for water, we shall give her milk
If she asks for a saree we shall give her a *sehlu*[10]
The bride is still only young
We shall take good care of her.

The very real emotion experienced at this moment is shown in
the dirge-like quality of the music and the poignancy of the
imagery. The bride's family hopes that 'the flowers in her hair
will never go dry'; they express sorrow at her departure – 'the
walls of the house where you grew up and played will weep'.
Informants wept openly when singing these songs, even though
theirs was a performance for the tape-recorder and totally out of
context. By this point in the proceedings the rite of passage has
fulfilled its purpose and incorporation has been achieved.

6. Wedding songs as social commentary

6.1 Wedding songs and social structure

Wedding songs provide interesting commentary and insight into
Gujarati social structure and social values, although this is by no
means the explicit function of the songs. Caste, for instance,
often occurs as a focus, particularly in *fatana*. In one song sung
by the bride's party, the groom's family are compared with lower-

caste members, considered inferior because they do manual work:

> The bridegroom's grandmother will have to be called a weaver
> Your paternal uncle will have to be called a goldsmith . . .
> Your maternal uncle will have to be called a cobbler . . .
> Your older brother will have to be called a watch-maker.

In another song the groom is presented as lowly because he is willing to associate with members of lower castes:

> Boom! Boom! The drums are beating, the bridegroom's
> party are entering the village.
> As they approach they pass the cobbler's yard. The groom
> sits with the cobbler and has soon learnt to mend shoes . . .
> As they approach they pass the kitchen. The groom sits
> with the cook and has soon learnt to cook . . .
> As they approach they pass sweepers. The groom talks with
> them and is soon sweeping the streets . . .
> As they approach they pass the toothbrush seller. The groom
> talks to him and is soon selling brushes.

Another prominent theme is family obligations and responsibilities. It is clearly the father's duty, for instance, to exercise wisdom and judgement in the choice of a husband for his daughter and, if necessary, to make financial sacrifices to ensure a good match. The father who does not take such responsibility seriously is pilloried, albeit indirectly and in a way which reflects just as badly on the groom in the following:

> Sir, what have you done, what have you done,
> What have you done? You have got an artificial pearl.
> You brought up your daughter with so much love and affection,
> Educated her and made her sophisticated, and then you
> gave her away to a stupid man.

The proper course of action is asserted equally strongly in the retort of the groom's party:

> Sir, you have done well, you have done a
> kindness, you have a real pearl.
> You brought up your daughter with so much love and affection,
> Educated her and made her sophisticated, and then you
> Gave her away to clever, intelligent man.

Traditionally, when a daughter married she no longer belonged to her parental family. Her home was with her husband and whether she was sad or happy that was where she belonged. In many cases, this separation was more than theoretical. To this day, according to some of my informants, there are isolated incidences of a daughter-in-law not being allowed to visit her family, though such cases are rare. Mostly the two families meet on many social occasions and certain events necessitate the presence of a married daughter and her husband. In weddings, for instance, the best man is always the sister's husband. The symbolic – and sometimes real – passage of a woman from one family to another is clearly charted in song:

> My dear sister, as you go to your in-law's house,
> Think of your mother-in-law as your own mother from now on
> Think of your husband's paternal uncle as your own paternal uncle
> Think of your husband's maternal uncle as your own maternal uncle
> Think of your husband's maternal uncle's wife as your own maternal uncle's wife
> Think of your husband's brother as your own brother
> Think of your husband's brother's wife as your own brother's wife.

The precarious status of the new daughter-in-law in her husband's household is also mentioned quite explicitly. In her position as the most junior female, the most menial tasks will automatically fall to her and there is nothing which her own family or even her husband can do to protect her interests:

> *Dham! Dham! Dham! Dham!*[11] *Sambhelu*[12]
> For generations it has been used to break the daughter-in-law
> If stones are found in the wheat my husband's sister will be angry.
> As the *channa*[13] expands in water so do my mother-in-law's demands expand
> The force with which the popcorn explodes can be compared with my Jethani's temper tantrums against me . . .

The bride's lot is an extremely ambivalent one. On the one hand, she is fulfilling social expectations and taking on a role for which she has been very well prepared. On the other hand, she feels she is taking leave of her own family and exposing herself to the not always benevolent authority of her in-laws. The reflection of a sister on such an occasion can be easily appreciated:

> None of your friends can say whether the tears are for joy or pain. Sister, may we never have to see you unhappy. Daughters are only held in trust.

6.2 Wedding songs and social values
A number of social values emerge as important in wedding songs. Men are expected to be strong, firm and the masters in their own home. Kishore Bhai, for instance, is mocked for tolerating the whims and extravagances of his bride and is given advice in no uncertain terms as to what he should do:

Kishore Bhai went to Bombay, oh the sulking of a spoilt woman.
His wife Hemleta desires expensive sarees, oh . . .
Kishore Bhai travelled all over Bombay but could not find any
suitable sarees, oh . . .
Kishore Bhai asked his friend to show him the way out of his
difficulties, oh . . .
The friend advised him to order some bamboo and have a cane
made, oh . . .
The cane goes swish, swish and the lady's desire for sarees
vanishes, oh . . .

Effeminacy and weakness cannot be tolerated at any price as
the following, albeit exaggerated, account makes clear:

Bridegroom, why is your best man like this?
If you look at his nose you see a jewel.
If you look at his ears you see earrings.
If you look at his mouth he stammers.
If you look at his hands you see bangles.
If you look at his hands you see bracelets.
If you look at his feet, you see sandals.
If you look at his legs he seems to be lame.

Women, in contrast, are expected to be respectful and
obedient. One song compares daughters with cows (the ultimate
symbol in Hindu folklore of long-suffering tolerance), 'going
wherever they are led' and encouraged to be a 'shadow' of their
husband. They are also told to respect in-laws and 'fall at their
feet'.

Sophistication, however, is seen as a desirable characteristic in
both the bride and the bridegroom. It is defined in terms of
clothing and possessions; it is also closely linked with education
and a certain degree of Westernisation. Sophistication is also a
highly valued family trait, as we see in the unabashed mockery
of Kokila's father. He is a simple man and, in contrast to the
bride's father-in-law, who arrives with a trunk of rupees and a
sackful of guineas, brings a cart full of carrots, a bag of onions
and a cart of aubergines.

However, generosity rather than sophistication emerges as the
most important family quality. Frequent references occur in
songs to the penny-pinching and miserly ways of the other side,
underlying the significance universally attached to this aspect of
social conduct.

I thought that the new *vevai* was worth one *lakh*.
It turns out he is worth 1 1/4 *lakh*.
I thought he would give me a *selu* but he fell short of giving me a
molia[14]

I thought that the new *vevan* was worth one *lakh*.
It turns out she is worth 1 1/4 *lakh*
I thought she would give me a *selu*, but she fell short of giving me a *sadi*[14]
I thought she would give me guineas, but she fell short of giving me rupees.

6.3 Modernity and tradition

There is clearly a need to exercise some caution in the social interpretation of wedding songs. Certain songs are a re-affirmation of traditional values which are today largely redundant. Songs which relate to the status of the bride in her husband's household, for instance, have more of a symbolic than real significance if the bride and groom are setting up their own household as is often the case. Similarly, the farewell songs point to a far more complete and dramatic breaking of ties with the bride's family than is usually the case.

However, this does not in any way imply that wedding songs invariably represent a petrified past with no significance for the contemporary Gujarati family. Extremely modern touches are also to be found and stand in marked contrast to the more traditional concepts and imagery. There is often a tangible tension between tradition and progress, accentuated in the song below, for instance, by the use of English 'rockets' and 'driving a car' in the Gujarati text.

In the cloudy skies the rockets fly
And look at the world below
Sirisbhai of today is driving round in a car
Whilst uneducated Dakshaben is still learning her letters
Sirisbhai of today wears a watch
Whilst uneducated Dakshaben goes around asking the time
Sirisbhai of today reads the newspapers
Whilst uneducated Dakshaben goes around asking the news.

The ancient tradition of wedding songs thus shows encouraging signs of adaptability to social change and faithfully reflects the tension which change inevitably generates.

7. Conclusion

The present study of wedding songs allows us to confirm a number of conclusions about the nature of Gujarati-speaking communities in Britain which have been suggested by purely anthropological research, and permits additional insights into these communities. The picture of social life reflected in wedding songs needs, admittedly, to be interpreted with caution. These songs are often extremely conservative in tone and sometimes reflect aspects of culture which are largely relics of the past. However, they also point to the changes which have taken place and the pressures placed on traditional values (both in India and among overseas Indians) by exposure to a Western lifestyle. Caste, for instance, appears to continue playing an important role in the selection of marriage partners and this aspect of social organisation goes on largely unchanged, whether or not formal links with India have been retained.

The singing of wedding songs in Britain would not appear to be as firmly institutionalised as it is either in East Africa or in India and there is certainly a growing tendency towards the playing of taped music. Can we therefore assume that wedding songs are simply a dying element of Gujarati oral culture? Very few Gujarati girls of school age, for instance, seem to know the songs and it would therefore be easy to conclude that they will not continue into the next generation. Yet wedding-song skills have always been selective: they are usually associated with older rather than younger women and not everyone is considered to be a 'good singer'. The continuing prestige associated with 'good singers', together with the feeling that they serve a valuable function in the context of a wedding, suggests that these songs may well survive for the foreseeable future. Nor should we overlook the growth of interest in Gujarati language and culture after the period of relative apathy which followed on early migration to Britain (see, for example, Wilding 1982; Linguistic Minorities Project 1985).

Perhaps the most important reason for optimism in the continuing tradition of wedding songs, however, is the vital social function which they fulfil. They provide a total framework which eases the transition of bride and groom from their unmarried states. They bring together a family, re-asserting their group identity. Most critical, they provide a very valuable release mechanism for the considerable tension generated during the preparation and celebration of marriage. The value of channelling universal emotions into highly formalised rites of this kind can seem particularly appealing to those of us who belong to a culture that has no such outlet.

We are left with the question as to why wedding songs, though passively known by the whole community, are formally and traditionally the province of women. It seems to us that, while marriage impinges on all members of the community, the practical and emotional implications for women are arguably of greater moment. It is therefore understandable that women, rather than men or mixed groups, should seek the release offered by the songs. The turning upside down of the accepted norms of social behaviour before firmly re-asserting the old order is particularly powerful when expressed by those members of society who traditionally exert least influence in formal settings. It is also understandable that women in their traditional role of mediators, rather than men, or mixed groups, be the channel for the social and cultural messages transmitted by the songs.

Notes

1. The research on which this chapter was based was made possible by a grant from the British Academy. We also wish to acknowledge the invaluable assistance of Chandra Katbamna in the translation and interpretation of the songs; and the helpful insight offered by Yasmin Thébault and Safder Alladina.
2. Ismailis form the most numerous Moslem Gujarati community in Britain. They are descendants of converted Lohana Hindus who accept the Aga Khan as their spiritual leader.
3. Husband's elder brother.
4. Incarnation of god on earth.
5. Jeth's wife.
6. Rama's wife. Rama and Sita represent the distillation of every perfection in their respective sexes.
7. Groom's/bride's father.
8. Money, but used here to refer to his warmth and kind position, not to his monetary wealth.
9. Groom's/bride's sister.
10. An expensive saree, usually in silk with fine gold embroidery.
11. An onomatopoeic word.
12. The tool used for pounding wheat into flour.
13. Chick pea which doubles its size on absorbing water.
14. An everyday saree.

Appendix

Transcription notation

Extended square brackets mark overlap between utterances, e.g.:

A: he's going to the ⌈ funeral
B: ⌊ oh my god

An equals sign at the end of one speaker's utterance and at the start of the next utterance indicates the absence of a discernible gap, e.g.:

A: after all she's dead =
B: =mm

Pauses are indicated by (.) (short) or (−) (longer).

Double round parentheses indicate that there is doubt about the accuracy of the transcription:

A: she lived in Brisbane, ((they were at Brisbane))

Where material is inaudible or impossible to make out, it is represented as follows:

A: but sorry ((xxx))

Single round parentheses give clarificatory information, e.g.:

A: he's dead, isn't he (laughs).

Material in square brackets is phonetic, e.g.:

A: the [θɨ] the theory goes

Underlining indicates that words are uttered with added emphasis, e.g.:

A: then they'd know that you hadn't come.

A small cross indicates the end of a tone-group, eg:

A: I'll never get out +

The symbol (pp) precedes words where the speaker speaks very quietly, e.g.:

A: (pp) I don't know

References

ABRAHAMS, R. (1972a) 'The training of the man of words in talking sweet', *Language in Society* **1** (1), 15–30.

ABRAHAMS, R. (1972b) 'Joking: the training of the man of words in talking broad' in T. Kochman (ed.), *Rappin' and Stylin' Out*. University of Illinois Press, Chicago.

ABRAHAMS, R. (1975) 'Negotiating respect: patterns of presentation among black women' in C. R. Farrar (ed.), *Women in Folklore*. University of Texas Press, Austin.

ALLADINA, S. (1986) 'Black people's language in Britain – a historical and contemporary perspective', *Journal of Multilingual and Multicultural Development* **7** (5), 349–60.

ALLEYNE, M. (1971) 'The cultural matrix of creolisation' in Hymes (ed.), 169–86.

ANSHEN, F. (1969) 'Speech variation among Negroes in a small southern community', unpublished PhD thesis, New York.

ARDENER, S. (1975) Introduction to S. Ardener (ed.) *Perceiving Women*. Malaby Press, London.

ARDENER, S. (1978) 'The nature of women in society' in S. Ardener (ed.), *Defining Females*. Croom Helm, London.

ARIES, E. (1976) 'Interaction patterns and themes of male, female and mixed groups', *Small Group Behaviour* **7** (1), 7–18.

BAUMANN, M. (1976) 'Two features of "women's speech"?' in B. L. Dubois & I. Crouch (eds), *The Sociology of the Languages of American Women*, Papers in Southwest English IV. Trinity University, San Antonio.

BEATTIE, G. W. (1981) 'Interruption in conversational interaction, and its relation to the sex and status of the interactants', *Linguistics* **19**, 15–35.

BEATTIE, G. W. (1983) *Talk: an analysis of speech and non-verbal behaviour in Conversation*. Open University Press, Milton Keynes.

BERNARD, J. (1972) *The Sex Game*. Atheneum, New York.

BLACK PEOPLES' PROGRESSIVE ASSOCIATION AND REDBRIDGE COMMUNITY

RELATIONS COUNCIL (1978) *Cause for Concern.*

BLAKE, C. F. (1979) 'Death and abuse in marriage laments: the curse of Chinese brides', *Asian Folklore Studies* **37**, 13–33.

BLOM, J. & J. GUMPERZ (1972) 'Social meanings in linguistic structures: code-switching in Norway' in J. Gumperz & D. Hymes (eds), *Directions in Sociolinguistics*. Holt, Rinehart & Winston, New York.

BRAH, A. (1978) 'South Asian teenagers in Southall: their perceptions of marriage, family and ethnic identity', *New Community* **6** (3), 197–206.

BROWN, C. (1984) *Black and White Britain*. Policy Studies Institute, London.

BROWN, G. (1977) *Listening to Spoken English*. Longman, London.

BROWN, H. R. (1969) *Die Nigger, Die*. Dial Press, New York.

BROWN, P. (1980) 'How and why are women more polite: some evidence from a Mayan community' in McConnell-Ginet, Borker & Furman (eds), 111–36.

BROWN, P. & S. LEVINSON (1978) 'Universals in language usage: politeness phenomena' in E. Goody (ed.), *Questions and Politeness*. Cambridge University Press, Cambridge, 56–310.

BYRNE, E. M. (1978) *Women and Education*. Tavistock Publications, London.

CAMERON, D. (1985) *Feminism and Linguistic Theory*. Macmillan, Basingstoke.

CHAMBERS, J. K. & P. TRUDGILL (1980) *Dialectology*. Cambridge University Press, Cambridge.

CHESHIRE, J. (1982) *Variation in an English Dialect*. Cambridge University Press, Cambridge.

CHIN, W. & S. SIMSOVA (1981) *Information sheets on Chinese readers*, Research Report no. 7. School of Librarianship, Polytechnic of North London.

CLARRICOATES, K. (1983) 'Classroom interaction' in J. Whyld (ed.), *Sexism in the Secondary Curriculum*. Harper & Row, New York.

COATES, J. (1986) *Women, Men and Language*. Longman, London.

COATES, J. (1987) 'Epistemic modality and spoken discourse', *Transactions of the Philological Society*, 110–131.

CONKLIN, N. F. (1973) 'Perspectives on the dialects of women' (cited in Thorne & Henley (eds), 1975), 251.

CROSBY, F. & L. NYQUIST (1977) 'The female register: an empirical study of Lakoff's hypothesis', *Language in Society* **6**, 313–22.

DALPHINIS, M. (1985) *Caribbean and African Languages: social history, language, literature and education*. Karia Press, London.

DE CAMP, D. (1971) 'Towards a generative analysis of a post-creole continuum' in Hymes (ed.)

DEEM, R. (1978) *Women and Schooling*. Routledge & Kegan Paul, London.

DELAMONT, S. (1980) *Sex Roles and the School*. Methuen, London.

DE LANGE, D . & B. KOSMIN (1979) *Community Resources for a Community Survey*. Research of the Board of Deputies of British Jews, London.

DELPHY, C. (1981) 'Women in stratification studies' in H. Roberts (ed.), *Doing Feminist Research*. Routledge & Kegan Paul, London.

DEUCHAR, M. (1983) 'I never done it', review of J. Cheshire *Variation in an English Dialect*, *THES* 19 (August).

DOUGLAS-COWIE, E. (1978) 'Linguistic code-switching in a Northern Irish village: social interaction and social ambition' in P. Trudgill (ed.), *Sociolinguistic Patterns in British English*. Edward Arnold, London.

DRIVER, G. (1980) 'How West Indians do better at school (especially the girls)', *New Society* 17 (January), 111–14.

DUBOIS, B. L. & I. CROUCH (1975) 'The question of tag questions in women's speech: they don't really use more of them, do they?', *Language in Society* 4, 289–94.

DUBOIS, B. L. & I. CROUCH (eds.) (1976) *The Sociology of the Languages of American Women*, Papers in Southwest English IV, Trinity University, San Antonio.

EAKINS, B. & G. EAKINS (1976) 'Verbal turn-taking and exchanges in faculty dialogue' in Dubois & Crouch (eds).

EDELSKY, C. (1981) 'Who's got the floor?' *Language in Society* 10, 383–421.

EDWARDS, D. (1980) 'Patterns of power and authority in classroom talk' in P. Woods (ed.), *Teacher Strategies: exploration in the sociology of the school*. Croom Helm, London.

EDWARDS, V. (1979) *The West Indian Language Issue in British Schools*. Routledge & Kegan Paul, London.

EDWARDS, V. (1986) *Language in a Black Community*. Multilingual Matters, Clevedon, Avon.

EDWARDS, W. (1984) 'Socialising the continuum: Guayanese sociolinguistic culture as social networks'. Paper presented to the 5th Biennial Conference of the Society for Caribbean Linguistics, Mona, Jamaica.

EHRENREICH, B. & D. ENGLISH (1979) *For her own Good: 150 years of the experts' advice to women*. Pluto Press, London.

ERICKSON, B. H. & T. A. NOSANCHUCK (1979) *Understanding Data*. Open University Press, Milton Keynes.

ERVIN-TRIPP, S. (1964) 'An analysis of the interaction of language, topic, and listener', *American Anthropologist* 66 (6; part 2), 86–102.

ESPOSITO, A. (1979) 'Sex differences in children's conversation', *Language and Speech*, 22 (3), 213–20.

FINNEGAN, R. (1970) *Oral Literature in Africa*. Clarendon Press, Oxford.

FISCHER, J. L. (1958) 'Social influences on the choice of a linguistic variant', *Word* 14, 47–56.

FISHMAN, P. M. (1977) 'Interactional shitwork', *Heresies* 2, 99–101.

FISHMAN, P. M. (1978) 'What do couples talk about when they're alone?' in D. Butturf & E. L. Epstein (eds), *Women's Language and Style*. Department of English, University of Akron.

FISHMAN, P. M. (1980) 'Conversational insecurity' in H. Giles, W. P. Robinson & P. Smith (eds), *Language: social psychological perspectives*. Pergamon, Oxford.

FISHMAN, P. M. (1983) 'Interaction: the work women do' in Thorne,

Kramarae & Henley (eds).

FRENCH, J. & P. FRENCH (1984) 'Gender imbalance in the primary classroom: an interactional account', *Educational Research* **26** (2), 127–36.

FULLER, M. (1983) 'Qualified criticism, critical qualifications' in L. Barton & S. Walker (eds), *Race, Class and Education*. Croom Helm, London, 166–90.

GAL, S. (1979) *Language Shift: Social Determinants of Language Change in Bilingual Austria*. Academic Press, New York.

GILES, H. (1973) 'Accent mobility: a model and some data', *Anthropological Linguistics* **15** (2), 87–105.

GILES, H. (1977) 'Linguistic differentiation in ethnic groups' in H. Tajfel (ed.), *Differentiation between Social Groups: studies in the social psychology of intergroup relations*. Academic Press, London, 361–86.

GILLIGAN, C. (1982) *In a Different Voice*. Harvard University Press, Cambridge, Mass.

GOFFMAN, E. (1967) *Interaction Ritual*. Anchor Books, New York.

GOODWIN, M. H. (1980) 'Directive–response speech sequences in girls' and boys' task activities' in McConnell-Ginet, Borker & Furman (eds), 157–73.

GRICE, H. P. (1975) 'Logic and conversation' in P. Cole & J. L. Morgan (eds), *Syntax and Semantics*, Vol. 3: *Speech Acts*. Academic Press, New York, 41–58.

GUMPERZ, J. (1982a) *Discourse Strategies*. Cambridge University Press.

GUMPERZ, J. (ed.) (1982b) *Language and Social Identity*. Cambridge University Press.

HALL, C. (1985) 'Private persons versus public someones: class, gender and politics in England, 1780–1850' in C. Steedman, C. Urwin & V. Walkerdine (eds), *Language, Gender and Childhood*. Routledge & Kegan Paul, London, 10–33.

HARRIS, S. (1984) 'Questions as a mode of control in magistrates' courts', *International Journal of the Sociology of Language* **49**.

HAUG, M. (1973) 'Social class measurement and women's occupational roles', *Social Forces* **52**.

HENRY, E. (1975) 'North Indian wedding songs', *Journal of South Asian Literature* **11**, 61–93.

HERSKOVITZ, M. (1937) *Suriname Folklore*. Oxford University Press, London.

HIRSCHMAN, L. (1973) 'Female–male differences in conversational interaction', paper presented to the Linguistic Society of America, Dec. 1973 (see abstract in Thorne & Henley (eds)).

HIRSCHMAN, L. (1974) 'Analysis of supportive and assertive behaviour in conversations', paper presented to the Linguistic Society of America, July 1974 (see abstract in B. Thorne & N. Henley (eds) 1975)).

HOLMES, J. (1984) 'Hedging your bets and sitting on the fence: some evidence for hedges as support structures', *Te Reo* **27**, 47–62.

HUDSON, R. (1975) 'The meaning of questions', *Language* **51**, 1–31.

HYMES, D. (ed.) (1971) *Pidginisation and Creolisation*. Cambridge University Press.

HYMES, D. (1971) 'On communicative competence', in J. B. Pride & J. Holmes (eds), *Sociolinguistics*. Penguin Books, Harmondsworth, 269–93.

JENKINS, L. & C. KRAMER (1978) 'Small group process: learning from women', *Women's Studies International Quarterly* 1, 67–84.

JENKINS, R. & B. TROYNA (1983) 'Educational myths, labour market realities' in B. Troyna & D. Smith (eds), *Racism, School and the Labour Market*. National Youth Bureau, Leicester, 5–16.

JESPERSEN, O. (1922) *Language: its nature, development and origin*. George Allen & Unwin, London.

JOHNSTON, T. F. (1975) 'The social meaning of Tsonga wedding songs', *Africana Marburgensia* 8 (2), 19–29.

JONES, D. (1980) 'Gossip: notes on women's oral culture' in C. Kramarae (ed.), *The Voices and Words of Women and Men*. Pergamon Press, Oxford, 193–8.

KALCIK, S. (1975) '". . . like Ann's gynecologist or the time I was almost raped". Personal narratives in women's rap groups', *Journal of American Folklore* 88, 3–11.

KEENAN, E. (1974) 'Norm-makers, norm-breakers: uses of speech by men and women in a Malagasy community' in R. Bauman & J. Sherzer (eds), *Explorations in the Ethnography of Speaking*. Cambridge University Press, Cambridge, 125–43.

LABOV, W. (1966) *The Social Stratification of English in New York City*. Georgetown University Press, Washington DC.

LABOV, W. (1972a) *Sociolinguistic Patterns*. University of Pennsylvania Press, Philadelphia.

LABOV, W. (1972b) *Language in the Inner City*. Basil Blackwell, Oxford.

LABOV, W. (1972c) 'Rules for ritual insults' in T. Kochman (ed.), *Rappin' and Stylin' Out*. University of Illinois Press, Chicago, 265–314.

LABOV, W., P. COHEN, C. ROBINS & J. LEWIS (1968) *A Study of the Non-standard English of Negro and Puerto Rican Speakers in New York City*. US Office of Education Co-operative Research Project 3288–1.

LADNER, J. (ed.) (1972) *Tomorrow's Tomorrow: the black woman*. Anchor Books, Garden City.

LAKOFF, R. (1973) 'The logic of politeness'. Papers from the Ninth Regional Meeting of the Chicago Linguistics Society, 292–305.

LAKOFF, R. (1975) *Language and Woman's Place*. Harper & Row, New York.

LEECH, G. (1983) *Principles of Pragmatics*. Longman, London.

LEET-PELLEGRINI, H. M. (1980) 'Conversational dominance as a function of gender and expertise' in H. Giles, W. P. Robinson & P. Smith (eds), *Language: social psychological perspectives*. Pergamon, Oxford, 97–104.

LEEWENBERG, J. (1979) *Cypriots in Haringey*. Research Report no. 1, School of Librarianship, Polytechnic of North London.

LE PAGE, R. B. & A. TABOURET-KELLER (1985) *Acts of Identity*. Cambridge University Press, Cambridge.

LEVINE, L. & H. CROCKETT (1966) 'Speech variation in a Piedmont community: postvocalic (r)' in S. Lieberson (ed.), *Explorations in Sociolinguistics*. Mouton, The Hague.

LINGUISTIC MINORITIES PROJECT (1985) *The Other Languages of England*. Routledge & Kegan Paul, London.

MACAULAY, R. K. S. (1977) *Language, Social Class and Education*. Edinburgh University Press.

MCCONNELL-GINET, S., R. BORKER & N. FURMAN (eds) (1980) *Women and Language in Literature and Society*. Praeger, New York.

MALTZ, D. N. & R. A. BORKER (1982) 'A cultural approach to male–female miscommunication' in Gumperz (ed.).

MARLAND, M. (1977) *Language across the Curriculum*. Heinemann, London.

MARTIN, F. (1954) 'Some subjective aspects of social stratification' in D. Glass (ed.), *Social Mobility in Britain*. Routledge & Kegan Paul, London.

MILROY, L. (1980) *Language and Social Networks*. Basil Blackwell, Oxford.

MILROY, L. (1987) *Observing and Analysing Natural Speech*. Basil Blackwell, Oxford.

MURRAY, O. (1985) 'Towards a model of members' methods for recognising interruptions', *Language and Society* 14, 31–40.

NEWBROOK, M. (1983) 'Sociolinguistic reflexes of dialect interference in West Wirral', PhD thesis, University of Reading.

NICHOLS, P. (1983) 'Linguistic options and choices for Black women in the rural South' in Thorne, Kramarae & Henley (eds).

NICHOLS, P. (1984) 'Networks and hierarchies: language and social stratification' in C. Kramarae, M. Schulz & W. O'Barr (eds) *Language and Power*. Sage Publications, Beverly Hills, California.

O'BARR, W. & B. ATKINS (1980) '"Women's language" or "powerless language"?' in S. McConnell-Ginet, R. Barker & N. Furman (eds).

ORTON, H. (1962) *Introduction to the Survey of English Dialects*. E. J. Arnold, Leeds.

PERKINS, M. (1983) *Modal Expressions in English*. Frances Pinter, London.

POP, S. (1950) *La Dialectologie: aperçu historique et methodes d'enquêtes linguistiques*. Université de Louvain.

POPLACK, S. (1980) 'Sometimes I'll start a sentence in English Y TERMINO EN ESPAÑOL: towards a typology of code-switching', Centro Working Papers, CUNY: Centro de Estudios Puertoriqueños.

RADCLIFFE-BROWN, A. (1952) *Structure and Function in Primitive Society*. Cohen & West, London.

RAMPTON, A. (1981) *West Indian Children In Our Schools* (Interim Report of the Committee of Inquiry into the Education of Children from Ethnic Minority Groups). HMSO, London.

REISMAN, K. (1974) 'Contrapuntal conversation in an Antiguan village' in R. Bauman & J. Sherzer (eds), *Explorations in the Ethnography of Speaking*. Cambridge University Press, Cambridge.

ROMAINE, S. (1978) 'Postvocalic (r) in Scottish English: sound change in progress?' in P. Trudgill (ed.), *Sociolinguistic Patterns in British English*. Edward Arnold, London.

ROMAINE, S. (ed.) (1982) *Sociolinguistic Variation in Speech Communities*. Edward Arnold, London.

RUSSELL, J. (1982) 'Networks and sociolinguistic variation in an African urban setting' in Romaine (ed.).

SACKS, H., E. SCHEGLOFF & G. JEFFERSON (1974) 'A simplest systematics for the organisation of turn-taking in conversation', *Language* **50**, 696–735.

SADKER, M. & D. SADKER (1985) 'Sexism in the schoolroom of the 80s', *Psychology Today* (March 1985), 54–7.

SANKOFF, D. (1980) *The Social Life of Language*. University of Pennsylvania Press, Philadelphia.

SCHEGLOFF, E. (1972) 'Sequencing in conversational openings' in J. Gumperz & D. Hymes (eds), *Directions in Sociolinguistics*. Holt, Rinehart & Winston, New York.

SEBBA, M. (1986) 'London Jamaican and Black London English', in D. Sutcliffe & A. Wong (eds).

SHUY, R., W. WOLFRAM & W. K. RILEY (1967) 'Linguistic correlates of social stratification in Detroit speech', US Office of Education, Washington DC.

SINGH, R. (1979) *Sikhs in Bradford*. Bradford College.

SMITH, D. (1976) *The Facts of Racial Disadvantage*. Political & Economic Planning, London.

SMITH, P. (1985) *Language, the Sexes and Society*. Basil Blackwell, Oxford.

SOSKIN, W. F. & V. P. JOHN (1963) 'The study of spontaneous talk' in R. Barker (ed.), *The Stream of Behaviour*. Appleton-Century-Crofts, New York.

SPENDER, D. (1982) *Invisible Women: The Schooling Scandal*. Writers and Readers Publishing Cooperative Society, London.

STONE, M. (1980) *The Education of the Black Child in Britain: the Myth of Multicultural Education*. Fontana, London.

STRODTBECK, F. & R. MANN (1956) 'Sex role differentiation in jury deliberations', *Sociometry* **19**, 3–11.

SUTCLIFFE, D. (1982) *British Black English*. Basil Blackwell, Oxford.

SUTCLIFFE, D. & A. WONG (eds.) (1986) *Language and the Black Experience*. Basil Blackwell, Oxford.

SWACKER, M. (1975) 'The sex of the speaker as a sociolinguistic variable' in Thorne & Henley (eds).

SWANN, J. & GRADDOL, D. (1988) 'Gender inequalities in classroom talk', *English in Education*, **22** (1), 48–65.

TANNEN, D. (1982) 'Ethnic style in male-female conversation' in Gumperz (ed.).

TANNEN, D. (1984) *Conversational Style: Analysing Talk among Friends*. Ablex, Norwood, New Jersey.

TANNEN, D. (1987) *That's Not What I Meant*. Dent, London.

TAYLOR, D. (1980) 'Ethnicity and language: a social psychological perspective' in H. Giles, W. P. Robinson & P. M. Smith (eds),

Language: Social Psychological Perspectives. Pergamon, Oxford, 133–9.

THOMAS, B. (1982) 'Fieldwork problems in a Welsh Valley community', *Cardiff Working Papers in Welsh Linguistics* **2**, 53–72.

THOMAS, B. (1987) 'Accounting for language shift in a South Wales mining community', *Cardiff Working Papers in Welsh Linguistics* **5**, 55–100.

THORNE, B. & N. HENLEY (eds), (1975) *Language and Sex: difference and dominance*. Rowley House, Newbury, Massachusetts.

THORNE, B., C. KRAMARAE & N. HENLEY (eds), (1983) *Language, Gender and Society*. Newbury House, Rowley, Massachusetts.

TINKER, H. (1977) *The Banyan Tree. Overseas Emigrants from India, Pakistan and Bangladesh*. Oxford University Press, Oxford.

TOMLINSON, S. (1984) *Home and School in Multicultural Britain*. Batsford, London.

TRUDGILL, P. (1972) 'Sex, covert prestige and linguistic change in the urban British English of Norwich', *Language in Society* **1**, 179–95.

TRUDGILL, P. (1974a) *The Social Differentiation of English in Norwich*. Cambridge University Press.

TRUDGILL, P. (1974b) *Sociolinguistics: an introduction*. Penguin Books, Harmondsworth.

TRUDGILL, P. (1978) 'Sociolinguistics and sociolinguistics' in P. Trudgill (ed.), *Sociolinguistic Patterns in British English*. Edward Arnold, London.

TRUDGILL, P. (1983) *On Dialect: social and geographical perspectives*. Basil Blackwell, Oxford.

UPADHYAYA, H. (1970) 'Some aspects of Indian marriage in Bhojpuri folksongs: Selection of mates', *Southern Folklore Quarterly* **34**, 116–26.

UPADHYAYA, S. P. (1973) 'Marriage songs of South Kanara: rituals and humour reflected in them', *Folklore International Monthly* **XIV** (August), 248–92.

URWIN, C. (1985) 'Constructing motherhood: the persuasion of normal development' in C. Steedman, C. Urwin & V. Walkerdine (eds), *Language, Gender and Childhood*. Routledge & Kegan Paul, London.

VAN GENNEP, A. (1960) *The Rites of Passage*. Routledge & Kegan Paul, London.

WELLS, G. (1979) 'Variation in child language' in V. Lee (ed.), *Language Development*. Croom Helm, London.

WELLS, J. (1973) *Jamaican Pronunciation in London*. Publications of the Philogical Society, Basil Blackwell, Oxford.

WEST, C. (1984) 'When the doctor is a lady', *Symbolic Interaction* **7** (1), 87–106.

WEST, C. & D. ZIMMERMAN (1977) 'Women's place in everyday talk: reflections on parent–child interaction', *Social Problems* **24**, 521–9.

WEST, C. & D. ZIMMERMAN (1983) 'Small insults: a study of interruptions in cross-sex conversations between unacquainted persons', in Thorne, Kramarae & Henley (eds).

WHYTE, J. (1986) *Girls into Science and Technology: the story of a project*. Routledge & Kegan Paul, London.

WILDING, J. (1982) *Ethnic Minority Languages in the Classroom? A Survey of Asian Parents in Leicester*. Leicester Council for Community Relations and Leicester City Council.

WODAK, R. (1981) 'Women relate; men report: sex differences in language behaviour in a therapeutic group', *Journal of Pragmatics* 5, 261–85.

ZIMMERMAN, D. & C. WEST (1975) 'Sex roles, interruptions and silences in conversation' in Thorne & Henley (eds).

Index